From My Mind, From My Voice

Tehron Jaqui Bush

Contents

Special Thank You To;

Marissa Lynn Bush

Cayden Price Worley

Delaney Kathryn Worley-Bush

Deloris Desery Bush

Ronald Anthony Bush

Cheryl Lynn Worley

James Burke Worley

Willie Henry Brown

Rosemary Brown

Norma Brown

Stephone Brown

Is Religion Important?

I am writing this chapter about a survey that pertains to the following quote: "Social life affects religion, and religion affects social life." I have attempted to find out exactly how religion and social life interact with friends, coworkers, classmates, the public, and family. I feel that these interactions of peers together make up the foundation of peer-to-peer communication. I will break down each question to my intention of religious and social interaction with my findings in conclusion.

Question #1: Do you think about your religion when you are with your friends?

This question was intended to get insight into observing the length relationships last concerning religion. I am wondering how long relationships last when conversations get based upon a religious preference. Are the most complicated relationships of friends, co-workers, classmates, or even family built around religion?

Question #2: Do you introduce religious prose when socializing?

Whether one may feel excited, happy, nervous, or sad, what is the frequency of religious voice being used to make decisions? Another question could be, do you trust someone who mentions religion in a conversation? I am wondering if religion is used to break social barriers. Do we use introduce religion for reassurance?

Question #3: Do you choose your friends according to your religion?

Many people outside of school or sports team may very well choose their peers based upon their church or religious preference. I intended on finding a relation to membership among peers that dug more in-depth than the surface peer-to-peer daily interaction. For example, some peers may or may not build a more profound relational affinity with each other when it is religion-based.

Questions #4: Do you feel challenged if you meet someone who is not of your religion?

How should one feel when being introduced to a potential friend who is of a different religion? If one is not of the traditional Christian faith, should one feel upset or discouraged or vice versa? Should one attempt to convert the other? What is the official process for a meeting in this area?

Question#5: Has there been a time when you felt your religion lacked inclusion in social interaction?

This question aimed at neglect for one another. Has the interviewee ever been in a situation where he or she felt that his or her religion had gotten neglected? Has he or she been overlooked in a case where he or she felt that his or her opinion was substantial to the conversation or meeting?

Question #6: Do you believe in having your religion interact within your social life?

Not everyone feels that they are religious; however, I believe it is essential to have one's religion act in one's social life for the simple reason of social stability. This question aims at finding how necessary balance in religion is meant to be in social life.

Question #7: How much influence does your religion have on your social life?

Religion, in my opinion, should be fundamental in one's social life. When one is religious with friends, family, etc., one may make better decisions. If one is religious, then he or she may have an elevated moral experience over someone who is not religious.

Question #8: Are you religious?

To get accurate results, I think this question had to get mentioned. A lot of the probing can be eliminated merely by asking the interviewees if you are religious. If they were not religious, then one would know that religion does not interact in his or her social life.

Question #9: Are you social?

This question is similar to; are you religious. If one is not social with peers, then one could say that his or her religion does not interact with his or her social life. Since this question has a variation of answers, for example, one can be rarely social. Religion for him or her in society may not be needed.

Question #10: What is your religion?

After an interviewee answers a ten-question questionnaire, the survey allows the interviewer to synthesize the data. Different answers to this particular question may provide insight toward one's religious beliefs about religion affecting social life in contemporary time.

I have provided insight toward my questioning for this survey analysis. All in all, I believe that the statement based upon my statistical findings permit me to think that the idea that "religion affects social life, and social life affects religion," overall, is situational. My data says that five out of five Christians believe no other religion can intimidate them when primarily confronted with alien faiths or difference. All five interviewees believe that religion should affect one's social life, but interestingly enough, not all agree that religion entirely affects one's social life. Four out of five say they do not choose their friends based on religion. Furthermore, I do not think the four found their answers on a long-term relationship with non-Christians. Overall, I think for the five interviewed, religion is situational with social interaction.

Christian Instruction

In my judgment, Mark 16:9–20 is the most crucial passage within chapters nine to sixteen of Mark's Gospel. Three sequential events occur within the text that illustrates the importance of Mark 16:9–20— Jesus Appears to Thomas; The Great Commission; and Jesus Ascends into Heaven—these provide insight toward the most important examples of the power that Jesus taught and bestowed to His followers.

After Jesus's crucifixion, He resurrects himself and appears to his eleven disciples during a meal. Mark chapter 16:14 presents Jesus rebuking his disciples for their unbelieving attitudes toward His appearance to the public after His resurrection. For example, Mark 9:12 states, "Elijah is indeed coming first to get everything ready. Why do the Scriptures say that the Son of Man must suffer greatly and get treated with utter contempt? But I tell you, Elijah had already come, and they chose to abuse him, just as the Scriptures predicted." This passage reveals that Jesus fulfilled the prophecy in addition to proving that Jesus provided insight of His almighty power in Mark 16:14. Immediately after that, Jesus states in Mark 9:31, "The Son of Man is going to get betrayed into the hands of his enemies. He will get killed, but three days later he will rise from the dead." Even though he foretold his disciples about His death and His resurrection, the disciples failed to acknowledge His supreme omnipotence. In contrast to their belief, The New Living Translation Bible footnotes that describes early manuscripts that claim Mark 16:14 includes the disciple's acknowledgment of His omnipotence. The disciples responded when Jesus appeared to them.

After Jesus demonstrates His omnipotence, He leaves His followers with the great message. The Great Commission is an essential passage in chapters nine to sixteen of Mark's Gospel because Jesus's message is the last request He had for not only His disciples but all of His followers. Jesus preaches "Go into the entire world and preach the Good News to everyone. Anyone who believes and gets baptized will get saved. But anyone who refuses to believe will be condemned. These miraculous signs will accompany those who believe: They will cast out demons in my name, and they will speak in new languages. They will be able to handle snakes with safety, and if they drink anything poisonous, it won't hurt them. They will be able to place their hands on the sick, and they will get healed." Jesus's teachings get summarized in this passage. After His resurrection, Jesus preaches that all who believe in Him will be rewarded with these special powers according to their faith.

In Mark 16:15–18, Jesus holds His followers accountable with a considerable amount of information. For example, Jesus says, "Go into the entire world and preach the Good News to everyone." This message is valuable because Jesus desires for Christianity to spread worldwide. The fact that this is the first message of the sermon Jesus speaks indicates the magnitude of importance in His message.

Next, Jesus includes instructions for salvation. For example, He says, "Anyone who believes and gets baptized will be saved. But anyone who refuses to believe will be condemned." Jesus aims to instill both belief and ritualistic practices to receive salvation. It is only by this way that one can earn salvation. Christians receive instructions for redemption, and everyone who believes and demonstrates faith will get saved. This significance is the first time Christians receive instructions for salvation.

Following after that, Jesus continues to preach. Jesus adds to His message by teaching "These miraculous signs will accompany those who believe…They will be able to place their hands on the sick, and they will be healed." These verses are relevant because, in them, Jesus orders his disciples to preach the Gospel. Before this, only the disciples had the power to cast out demons, to speak new languages, to handle snakes, and to heal the sick. This verse from the Book of Mark is essential because Jesus bestows power to his followers.

Jesus manifests His divine power when He ascends into heaven making Mark 16:19–20 an essential passage in chapters 9–16 of Mark's Gospel. For example, this passage states that "When the Lord Jesus had finished talking with them; he was taken up into heaven and sat down in the place of honor at God's right hand. The disciples went everywhere and preached, and the Lord worked through them, confirming what they said by many miraculous signs." The completion of His work is most significant when Jesus sits at the right hand of God. Mark 16:19 professes the authority of Jesus as God in the flesh. Mark 16:20 is also an important passage because "Mark's Gospel emphasizes Jesus's power as well as his servant-hood." For example, The New Living Translation provides commentary that supports Mark 16:20. "Jesus's life and teaching turned the world upside down. The world sees power as a way to gain control over others. Jesus, with all authority and power in heaven and on earth, chose to serve others. As believers, we are called to be servants of Christ. As Christ served, so we are to help. Jesus chose to serve, so Christians are to serve as well. Jesus's demonstration of power, teaching, and service are depicted by Mark 16:9–20, which is a small selection of essential passages in the Bible. In conclusion, Mark 16:9–20 is an integral part of Mark's Gospel.

Jesus provides clarity in Mark 16:9–20 for the mission of the Christian faith. Mark 16:9–20 is the most critical passage within chapters 9–16 of Mark's Gospel because Jesus provides insight toward His omnipotence, the transfer of power to His believers, and His authority as God in the flesh, where he sits at the right hand of God.

Love, Power, Betrayal
& Sub-ordinance

The Torah is a collection of five books, Genesis, Exodus, Leviticus, Numbers, and Deuteronomy. These five books are considered the Hebrew law. Moses gets regarded as the author of the Torah. The Torah was originally written in the Hebrew language and is also translated in English today. Theologians agree that the origin of the Torah dates back to 1280 BCE. Predominantly read in synagogues, the Torah gets chanted by a musical system called the trop. To learn from the Torah, one must be an adult. In the Hebrew faith, an adult is considered to be "13 years old and one day of age." When a child becomes an adult, a Bar Mitzvah or Bat Mitzvah is held to mark the age of adulthood.

The Torah gets made by a unique process. Even though the Torah gets published in both Hebrew and English, the scroll for ceremonial purposes is handwritten. A scribe hand writes the Torah. The process to which the scripture gets written takes as long as one year to complete. The scripture is comprised of kosher cattle skin, stretched and prepared on a wooden frame. Altogether the Torah contains 248 columns. One rectangle of parchment or scroll yields space for three to four columns. The Torah requires about eighty-plus skins to complete the scroll. Once complete, the scroll is called a Sefer Torah, which gets only used for ceremonial purposes. Since the parchment is very holy, one must use a pointer called *yad* when reading from the scroll. The synagogue maintains the scriptures that are kept in the ark. The ark is a cabinet, which refers to the Ark of the Covenant. The Ark of the Covenant is a holy place to store the scrolls in.

The Torah is essential to the Hebrew faith because it gets connected to the idea of teaching. Judaism claims to have the only revealed text by

God. The Torah has served as a paradigmatic revelation from God. The Torah stems from God's love to the will of Moses. The Torah bears the primary sense of teaching or instruction. The Torah refers to messages delivered from God in the form of auditory disclosures of the divine voice.

The central passage I choose from the Torah is the book of Genesis, describes the original story of the first man and the first woman, who are examples for young Hebrews to serve spiritual maturity. This passage illustrates examples of love, power, betrayal, and sub ordinance. Genesis chapter three demonstrates the story of Adam and Eve. Adam and Eve decided to be disobedient to God by succumbing to the serpent for their own will. This story is the first sin of man. The serpent coerces the woman to eat the fruit from the Tree of Life. The woman feeds the man the forbidden fruit to which God said, "You shall not eat of one of the trees of the garden?" Genesis 3:1. Since both the woman and man ate from the Tree of Life, together they understood good and evil; "Their eyes were opened" Genesis 3:7. God said unto them, "Where are you?" And the man said, "I heard your voice in the garden, and I was afraid because I am naked. So I hid." In Genesis 3:9–10, the man explained his disobedience to God. God became disappointed in both the woman and the man for their unbelieving attitudes in God's Word. Not only did the serpent receive punishment for his misbehavior, but the man and the woman were also punished. As punishment for both the man and the woman, God commanded that women will bear children in pain. Man shall work, and work shall be done in thorns and thistles. God provided a name for a man. The man was called Adam. The man provided a name for women. Adam named his wife Eve since she was "the mother of all life" Genesis 3:20. In the end, God placed a cherub to guard everyone against approaching the Tree of Life. This scripture is the story of Adam, Eve, and the first sin.

I believe the story of Adam and Eve is remarkable because it explains the creation of man and woman and the existence of sin. The original sin teaches that all humans sin. Travail in the universe is a reminder of Adam and Eve's original punishment. Genesis 3 illustrates companianship between man and woman. One can see a parallel between God's laws and governmental laws. For instance, when Adam and Eve ate the forbidden fruit, Genesis 3 taught Jews and Christians that rules are meant to adhere. Similarly, government laws such as traffic ordinances enforce the law for the productivity and safety of the public. Genesis 3 teaches Hebrews the laws of the land. Adam and Eve's story provides a reference for Hebrew followers to be obedient to both natural and governmental regulations.

The story of Adam and Eve expresses many values from the written text for modern society. Genesis 3:1–24 references themes of love, power, betrayal, and sub ordinance. Love can be seen when God loved his creation. He provided man with a place to eat and a place to live. God created woman whom Adam named Eve. Adam and Eve lived in a kingdom named Eden. Genesis 3:1–24 demonstrates the companionship between Adam, Eve, and God.

Genesis 3:1–24 presents the power and the struggle between good and evil. The serpent represented evil, while Adam and Eve personified good. The serpent deceived Eve, so she committed the first sin with Adam. The creation of Adam and Eve is said to be right in the image of God. Humans, therefore, are good but can commit acts of evil. We see examples of this in society today. For example, a man commits adultery against his wife. Their original relationship may have been right; however, the man has committed an act of evil against his wife. As a result, power gets exerted over the man, and he is likely to be punished. This example is equivalent to the sin of Adam and Eve. God exercised power over Adam and Eve by banishing them from the Garden of Eden.

The story of Adam and Eve also teaches Hebrews the theme of betrayal. The serpent, Adam, and Eve all commit sins. The serpent lies to Eve, Eve feeds Adam the forbidden fruit, and Adam hides from God. This event is important because it tells Hebrews about the free use of will in modern society. All three characters from the Hebrew text enact the will of God. This example aims to provide some insight into human behavior. The first sin is vital because original sin offers a reference toward human characteristics. Mortal sin and Human will always sin due to original sin introduced by Adam and Eve.

In the story of Adam and Eve, sub ordinance to God can be seen as practical. God created Adam and Eve in his image. Adam and Eve are subordinates to God. One can understand the idea of subordination concerning monotheism. In this passage, God has the power to love and to punish, and the Hebrews established in the Torah the idea of one God. Genesis 3:1–24 tells the story of humans answering to God. This relationship is essential because Hebrew religion presents humans as being subordinate. The highest power of authority has God being male in the Hebrew religion. The woman gets created for a man showing an idea of subordination in Hebrew society. One can see examples of this in modern societies today. Male figures hold high-paying positions and high-ranking positions.

In contrast, women get described as subordinates in the Hebrew Torah, which are steadily becoming more important in societies today. The ideas of subordination teach Hebrew followers to obey and to be obedient to God and authoritative figures in culture. The story of Adam and Eve is an excellent teaching tool to present the idea of original sin to young Hebrew followers. The sacred scrolls are vital because they teach new followers of Judaism, the tradition and values of Hebrew society. I chose the story of Adam and Eve to illustrate the ideas of love, power, betrayal, and sub ordinance as a window into modern society.

Civil Problem

The civil war in Sudan has lasted for more than two centuries, making it one of the longest civil conflicts in history. I will explain this conflict in detail and apply Kenneth Waltz's three levels of analysis: Who are the individual leaders or groups problems that led to war? What are the state regime problems that led them to war? What are the systemic factors that led to the Sudanese civil war?

Northern Sudan came under the rule of Egypt after 2600 BC. Missionaries converted northern Sudan into a Christian region during the sixth century AD quickly; Muslims conquered Egypt, which resulted in Arab Muslim control of Sudan. Then the Egyptians re-conquered Sudan. After the Egyptians' final conquest of Sudan, Britain declared Egypt an occupied territory. Therefore, Sudan was simultaneously ruled by both Egypt and Britain and was referred to as Anglo-Egyptian Sudan. Following up in 1953, Egypt and Britain granted Sudan the right of self-government and independence. Sudan has been in civil conflict for more than two centuries. Led by an Arab military officer, General Abboud, the government head, focused on applied Arabic and Islamic agenda for the entire state of Sudan. In 1958, General Abboud sanctioned Islamic law, which created the conditions that produced Sudan's civil war between the Arab Muslim north and the Christian south.

The tension between the Arab Muslim north and the Christian south was enough to require the introduction of the Addis Ababa Peace Agreement in 1975, which further touched on the emotions and the religion of the Christian south. The agreement stipulated that the state must honor both Islam and Christianity. However, neither Islam nor Christianity would be a state-sanctioned religion. This agreement temporarily ended the religious dissatisfaction between the north and the south. Around 1978, the government of Sudan began to reject them.

Peace agreement initially proposed by President General Abboud. A rebellious effort sparked for the second time in 1983 when the Arabic government attempted to transfer military members from the south to the north. As a response, two separate militant groups were formed— the National Islamic Front (NIF) and the Sudanese People's Liberation Army (SPLA). The conflict in Sudan is about defending Christian and Islamic beliefs, especially where they coexist geographically. At this point, Waltz's three theories are especially useful to consider how to indicate the conflict.

The feudalistic unrest between Sudan's Arab Muslim north and Christian south distinctly calls for attention to the disposition of the NIF and the SPLA. The NIF is the political organization that has been the most influential in the Sudanese government. It supports the maintenance of an Islamic state and rejects the concept of a secular state, which was the original intention of the Addis Ababa Agreement. The NIF has shown itself to be both politically astute and ruthless in its us of violence. Once the NIF bestowed power, the NIF intensified the war against the south to further its goal of Islamic fundamentalism. Islamic fundamentalism has always been the chief operating motive of the NIF about southern Sudan.

Without the adversarial forces of the SPLA, the NIF would achieve its objective. The SPLA is mostly a Christian Sudanese rebel movement and then became a more legitimate political party. Based in southern Sudan, it is fighting the civil war against the Sudanese government, which is represented by the NIF. The SPLA's declared aim is to establish a democratic Sudan with the SPLA as the leading party taking precedence in the southern region. A treaty has been negotiated between the SPLA and the NIF; however, the former has withdrawn from negotiation, while the latter led the government—again—similar to the Addis Ababa Peace Agreement, alleging violations of several conditions of the peace agreement. In conclusion, one can see in this case the first problem of national command.

There are state problems for the cause of war in Sudan according to Waltz's analysis. Let us focus on the political, humanitarian, and economic reasons why Sudan has failed. The citizens who have taken power by election or military means failed the people of Sudan, leading to the Sudanese civil war. Sudan's governmental policy put into motion has led to the uneven development of Sudan. Sudan's people are still living in poverty when most of the world lives very modernly. One could say most of Sudan's developmental problems stem from the lack of political, social, humanitarian, and economic rights. If its government can expedite these three factors of deficiency, then one could say and feel more comfortable that Sudan is on the right path. Humanitarian rights are and should be considered extremely important to Sudanese citizens and policymakers. Sudanese citizens, mainly the Christians, are fleeing their homes. The remaining ones have nothing more to eat. Millions of Sudanese citizens have died, and millions are suffering from famine. The Sudanese government is promoting a program of ethnic cleansing, which encourages Muslim citizens to destroy Christian citizen in the name of the governmental law. These are the Humanitarian problems Sudan continues to face. The Sudanese economy has been sparse due to the lack of a stable government and lack of a working class due to genocide—all attributed to the ongoing civil war. Even worse, Sudan's lack of rainfall has been profoundly affecting its cash crop economy. Sudan's political, humanitarian, and economic deficiencies have led its state into a civil war.

Nevertheless, Sudan proved that it is in a political, humanitarian, and economic crisis, which, according to Waltz, led to the Sudanese civil war. If Sudan had remained a territory of Egypt Pre-British colonization, maybe then it would have gained its independence, and Sudan would not be in a civil war. Any hope for Sudanese sovereignty has been prevented by British colonization and decolonization. When Britain integrated Sudan, British occupancy was supplemented by Egyptian diplomacy. Furthermore, together, a British and Egyptian policy created tension between Arabic Muslim north and Christian south Sudan. If it were not for Britain occupying Egypt, Sudan would have solely been under the control of Egyptian diplomacy. Interestingly, Britain executed its decolonization policy, and Sudan usurped independence post-colonization.

Post-colonization, the second systems example contributing to Sudan's civil unrest was its arms suppliers. As a consequence of a post-colonial environment, the lack of current stability allowed for northern and southern Sudan to need new military trainers and suppliers. The Soviet Union supplied the most significant numbers of weapons including tanks, aircraft, and artillery, while Egypt provided missiles and personnel carriers. The Republic of China provided some weapons alongside the United States. Waltz's three-step analysis aims to analyze the conflict to illustrate the causes of war. Sudan has conclusive results that indicate not only the cause and effect of the Sudanese war but also the need for help from the international system. The Sudanese conflict between the NIF and SPLA needs intervention to resolve the internal dispute. Sudan needs to rethink policy matter that aims to stimulate its economic and humanistic growth and, more importantly, develop and support the infrastructure of a healthy independent state, which it has lacked since its inception of independence.

Social Survey

I will identify answers for societal norms that illustrate responses to social life affecting religion and religion affecting social life in this questionnaire.

1. Is marriage the most important relational hierarchy socially or in your religion?

    This question is important because, for some people, marriage is the highest achievement in the social spectrum as well as in a religious spectrum. Depending on the society or the religion, one may either aim to stand out individually or embrace culture religiously.

2. Is it against your religion or your social norm to teach your children under the age of twenty-one how to use a gun?

    This question aimed at gun safety. How much risk gets associated with teaching a child how to use a handgun knowing it may be illegal depending upon where one lives. One could argue for safety and security in the operation of a handgun. Another may say for the use of a handgun for game hunting to provide food for the family to eat. Both address a level of goodness and also present a level of danger. When weighing the odds for decision making, what social or religious connections does one make?

3. Since you have good credit, your husband or wife (s) brother asks you to buy them a car. Socially, what do you do? Or what is your religious response?

How would one respond to a question of generosity? This person should get the feeling of being taken advantage of depending upon one's economic stability. Socially, the moral idea here is to be self-sufficient. Religiously, the idea here is to help a loved one.

4. At lunch, you and one thousand dollars lying on the bench in a brown lunch bag. No one sees you pick it up and look inside, socially what do you do? Or how does your religion influence your decision?

The importance of this question is to determine if the individual's goodness remains intact while in a demoralized society. A religious response could produce similar results and yet could have a more full-filling and emotional response too.

5. A close family member is terminally ill with cancer and is on life support. At age fifty-one, do you pull the plug? Socially, how do you respond? Or what is your religious response?

Socially, one would want to do the best thing for the common good. Pulling the plug could result in shortening another's life. On the other hand, a religious response could say that the ill family member is now going to be with his or her maker.

6. Your boss demands that you create a proposal before you leave work that day. You are running late, but your daughter has an evening wedding? Socially, what do you do? Or what does your religion deem to be appropriate action?

The person answering this question has to prioritize and balance their responsibilities. The two events are highly significant. The best common answer would be to do everything one could on the project, go to the wedding, and then come back and finish the project that evening. A person who chose to answer religiously would talk to his or her boss and let him know that their daughter is getting married that evening and that he or she requests a leave of absence for the festivity. This question poses a big dilemma for a social and religious response. Weighing options is the most crucial factor to this question.

7. The mailman personally hands you the mail, and you notice that there is an unexpected overpayment check for you. Do you call the company and inquire about it, or do you go and spend it? Socially, how do you respond to this question? Or religiously, how do you respond to this question?

Living in a demoralized nation, one could easily say it is the fault of the company. I will spend the check. One may consult his or her family before making the decision. One may put forth his or her moral foundation and return the check. The point of this question is to reach a common good for both the individual and the company.

8. You're a taxi cab driver, and you have a pregnant woman in the cab. You notice that your taxi is out of gas and that she has to deliver the baby immediately. Do you risk the trouble to get her to a hospital, or do you stop and ill up instead? Socially, how do you respond? Or what would your religious response be?

The question is: What is the greatest good for the baby? On the one hand, you could make it to the hospital. On the other, you could end up delivering a baby, which you have no experience. Would delivering the baby be socially accepted, or would you give it your best shot and attempt to make it to the hospital. The religious response would be to get the baby in the care of professionals. A social response would be to call an ambulance and provide the woman with the best care that you know.

9. Your son or daughter says they are gay. Do you tell them to join the church? How do you respond socially? Or what would your religion say about your situation?

There are groups and organizations that people can join in to express one's opinions or ideas. A social response would be for the child to join a group similar to them so that he or she could engage in healthy conversation. The church would not be the best answer for a response for advocacy of homosexuality; they instead act as a deterrent organization for the child. A religious response would minimize homosexuality, while a universal answer would be for the advocacy of homosexuality.

10. Before your dad died, he wrote you and your mother into the will. The bank releases the money to your mother, but she never gives it to you. Instead, she puts the money into a trust. Socially, how do you respond to your mother? Or what would a religious response to your mother include?

One may see that the social norm speaks against the mother collecting money in behalf of her daughter. The daughter is entitled to her share of the inheritance. Social norms say that the individual is entitled to whatever is in favor of the individual. Religiously, I think the mother has a plausible argument. The mother has believed to be correct on behalf of the child. She is protecting the child's best interest.

I have provided insights toward my questioning for this survey analysis. All in all, I believe that I have illustrated the separation between religious life and social life. Religion aims to unite the individual to universal law and fulfillment, while social norms aim for personal acceptance of moral ideas that help to maintain social order. Even though we live in a demoralized society, both religion and social life affect one another.

Global Affairs

T he United Nations is an international organization. It was founded in 1945 by former Secretary of State Cordell Hull, who won the Nobel Prize for his efforts in creating the institution consisting of fifty-one significant countries following World War II. The United Nations began and continues to develop programs and organizations for international peace, security, diplomatic relations among nations, social progress, living standards, and human rights. The United Nations as an international organization maintains powers from its charter to take action on global issues. Its conferences provide a forum for 192 member nations to offer a podium for them to express their views. The General Assembly, the Security Council, the Economic Council, the Social Council, and various other member committees compose the body of The United Nations.

The United Nations has provided a framework and support for global affairs. For them, peacekeeping has been the most influential branch of international service. However, the United Nations maintains other services such as conflict prevention, humanitarian assistance, sustainable development, environment, refugee protection, disaster relief, counter-terrorism, disarmament and non-proliferation of nuclear weapons, democracy and governance, and economic and social development. The United Nations is an organization that has a hand into everything. I will discuss in detail, five out of many conferences the United Nations hosts such as environment, women's rights, population control, weapons control, and terrorism. The United Nations is committed to improving international relations by covering the full range of human institution for the support of global progress, establishing it as an effective organization. Furthermore, I will also discuss three different problems—biotechnology, the Iraqi conflict, and the United Nations administration—that the committees lack resolve. These problems continue to have the need to be improved upon to further the organization's impeccable record of global politics.

After the United Nations Conference on the Human Environment in Stockholm, environmental management emerged as a meaningful discussion among nations in international relations. Scientific monitoring of ecological depletion cautions nation leaders to notice. Awareness of these conditions presents policymakers to build international legislation for environmental governance. Human-induced climate changes, relative rises in sea levels, and the global dispersion of organic pollutants are producing adverse effects on the global environment. Transboundary pollution of river waters, the collective numbers of migratory species, the impact of acid rain, impact the global climate. The loss of natural areas, pollution of urban air, contamination of drinking water and, diminishing supply of natural resources perpetuate the environmental problem globally. The United Nations Conference in Stockholm is where the nations began to build environmental committees with intentions of interdependence between cross-national agencies. "With growing experience and knowledge, nations came to realize that no one government alone could safeguard the environment and that international cooperation would need to be enhanced." Nations began to develop methods to evaluate environmental conditions. Their environmental agencies noticed that environmental conditions were depleting faster than previous statistical environmental knowledge. To resolve environmental deficiencies, the United Nations held its conference on the environment and the development. To continue its efforts, the United Nations held another conference of the World Summit on Sustainable Development. This conference held by the General Assembly committee desired to see improvement in the international environmental governance. Since then, various conferences became held. During a conference at UNCED, "A consensus had emerged that proactive management would be needed to sustain the air, water and other natural resources upon which the human economy depended upon." As a result of the UNCED conference, nations began to compartmentalize and focus on evolving their policies to evaluate environmental concerns and issues. Each nation began to assemble national legislation for environment control. "Constitutions were amended to provide the right to a balanced environment. Treaties were negotiated and ratified to establish regional and international standards." The United Nations foresaw a need to improve "systems of international environmental governance" and "recommended measures toward such systems."

The United Nations is an active organization for women's rights. At one conference, the slogan was "Human rights are women's rights, and women's rights are human rights." This remark is a new issue for the United Nations and its women. The conference attacked the issue of patriarchal privilege that allowed men to abuse, and even kill wives within the nuclear family under common law protection. In addition to but on a lighter note, the United Nations committee denies women's rights as their right to decide on how many children they wanted, no forced abortions, family planning, and inheritance rights to land and house. This conference provided provisional goals for stating that women should have "the equal right to inheritance" rather than "the right to equal inheritance." Shifts in world attitudes and changes to nation-state laws and practices are criteria to measure the success of United Nations organizations for women's rights. The United Nations women's rights committee chose to focus on family intervention for several reasons. Families who live in countries moving from planned economies and welfare states to reliance on market economies have a strain on the family during economic transition. Gender equality policy requires consideration of individuals within the family. Humanistic and feminist views of economics involve women and men as partners in the development process designed to construct a new society. The family is the basic unit for evaluation. The family is an evolving institution. The family provides support, security, and stability for society; however, women in these families are becoming oppressed. The destruction of the traditional family in the course of modernization is becoming delivered by an economic transition that lessens security for women without providing new institutional forms for that security. The United Nations is working on creating organizations for women support.

The United Nations is an active organization for population control. In the Programme of Action, the United Nations committee hosted the International Conference on Population and Development. The committee states that programs should enable individuals to plan the number of children, along with the individual preference of the time between each child. Services offered to families get established upon the decisions made in this conference. The United Nations cannot evaluate the value of its programs unless each family achieves their family planning desires based on a plan of action. The Program of Action committee has proactively established that families nationally have no quantitative factors for utilizing contraceptive methods to family planning. The ICPD program of motion states that "All countries should strive to make accessible through the primary care system and provide reproductive health to all individuals of appropriate ages as soon as possible and no later than the year 2015." This plan of action still maintains its value since the World Summit in 2005. The outcome, which supports the ICPD program, states that "We commit ourselves to achieve universal access to reproductive health by 2015, as a set out at the International Conference on Population and Development, integrating this goal in strategies to attain the internationally agreed development goals, including those contained in the Millennium Declaration aimed at reducing maternal mortality, improving maternal health, reducing child mortality, promoting gender equality, combating HIV/AIDS and eradicating poverty." Other improved coverage for family planning could surface from a robust United Nations consensus. Current international measurement of unmet need in survey analysis should serve as a starting point for national monitoring. The nations should monitor access to and of reproductive health services every three years.

The United Nations is an active organization for the ban to use cluster munitions. Cluster munitions are weapons incorporating numerous separate explosive sub-munitions or "bomblets." The United Nations convention will require parties not to use, develop, produce, acquire, stockpile, retain or transfer covered munitions, or assist parties doing so. The UN has determined that certain covered weapons allow retention and use of some newer "smart" weapons containing a small number of explosive sub-munitions. The UN has allowed for retention of limited stock for use in training for explosive ordinance disposal. The conference also states that nations have up to eight years to destroy existing stocks of proscribed weapons. Nations may apply for two additional periods of four years to destroy such weapons. This convention contains extensive provisions on identification and removal of unexploded sub-munitions in addition to the treatment and assistance to civilian victims of cluster munitions. The results of the conference stipulated that each nation shall notify the governments of all nations, not a party, to this convention and shall promote the norms the nation establishes that shall make its best efforts to discourage nations, not a party, to this Convention from using cluster munitions. Also, the United Nations provisions stipulate military personnel may engage in military cooperation and operations with nations, not a party, to this convention that might participate in activities prohibited by the United Nations. The United Nations advocates and places value on just and appropriate warfare. These provisions are relevant to the health and dignity of military personnel.

The United Nations is an effective organization after the creation and documentation of international policy based on terrorism. The Palermo convention based upon terrorism addressed issues such as human trafficking, migrant smuggling, and the illicit manufacturing and trafficking of firearms.

Parties of the convention have a choice to a model of participation that will be criminalizing at the national level that is a "conspiracy offense" or a "criminal association" offense. The definition provided by the United Nations Palermo Conference gets bound under international law for nations that ratified the convention and serves as authoritative guidance for the international community. Security of the international community is vital to the mission of the United Nations Council.

In discussing the effectiveness of the United Nations, it is not a perfect organization. The United Nations may have a hand in proactive leadership for international diplomacy; however, it can also be potentially disastrous. About biotechnology, peacekeeping, and administration, the United Nations has no active mitigation and correction for these issues.

The United Nations is ineffective about biotechnology. Global food prices have risen to 83 percent. This situation, combined with recent price increases, have contributed to the wave of food riots in countries as diverse as Haiti, Indonesia, Mexico, Bangladesh, Burkina Faso, Egypt, Senegal, Cameroon, Morocco, Yemen, Somalia, and the Philippines. These food riots with many millions of hungry, radicalized peasants and slum dwellers have caused the World Bank and the United Nations to react. The World Bank, which is a development of the United Nations, has foreseen critics that have long questioned its motives. Critics have attacked the conditions of the World Bank when it makes decisions about dispensing aid to poorer nations. The World Bank has failed due to the lack of international policy for food aid and the spiraling of oil prices. The United Nations has had a problem with providing alternative notions of agriculture development. During one conference, the United Nations agenda was not geared toward revitalizing local agriculture, protecting biodiversity, the health of consumers, and the earth's atmosphere. Instead of focusing on making trade fairer, restoring seed and grain banks, setting up marketing boards for local produce, agreeing on bio-fuel cultivation, and supporting land reform and setting up institutions to spread the accumulated knowledge of indigenous cultivators, the conference's declaration called for more production of and higher yields on agriculture. The United Nations did not use its time effectively. Instead of recognizing the systemic failures of the global market, it decided that better technology and investment could allow farmers to produce agriculture for consumers from the nutritional crisis.

Former Secretary of State Cordell Hull called the United Nations Charter "one of the great milestones in man's upward climb toward a truly civilized existence." Sixty years later, George W. Bush had done more to reverse the United Nations during a postwar period. The Iraqi War harmed not only the United Nations but also the dream of world governance and world peace. Roosevelt called the United Nations a "world organization for permanent peace." Now in the early years of the twenty-first century, Bush returns international relations to the raw power politics of the nineteenth century and enforced international law for the lawless. The United States is undeterred and focused on the current situation. It repudiates any willingness to allow the United Nations to act independently, and it refuses to accept a set of restraints derived from international law. A report adds, "In most States, including those most closely allied to the United States, over 70 percent of the public opposes U.S. Military action against Iraq." Even presidents who treated the United Nations with contemptuous disregard tried to conform to international norms."

We live in a unipolar world, you have the United States intent on pursuing a global dominance project, and there is no countervailing power. The Cold War, at least, had the general benefit of a countervailing force. States were not as dependent on the law. There is a greater dependence on international law in a unipolar world. The law did not bound Bush's actions. As a miss-directive by a key State such as the United States, gives other nations a clear indication that their self-interest lies not in taking issues to the United Nations but in establishing facts on the ground. Secretary of the State Colin Powell wrote, "Our fervent pursuit of war with Iraq is driving the United States to squander the international legitimacy that has been the United States most potent weapon of both offense and defense since the days of Woodrow Wilson. We have begun to dismantle the largest and most effective web of international relationships the world has ever known."

The lack of United States obedience to the international system negatively affected the United Nations in its use of soft power to correct and to guide the remaining nations on the issues of Iraq.

Despite its growth in aid implementing a global institution. The United Nations has continued to suffer from internal management and scandal, thus, hurting its international policy and reform. There is a particular need to place attention to the areas of management and administration. Management reform was seen by many as the most crucial element in overall United Nations reform. United Nations reform has been directly linked to financial resources in addition to future success, depending on its ability to adopt sustainable managerial and administrative diligence. The United Nations agenda has expanded tremendously in recent years, and its focus is no longer political or economic. Participating states have mandated the United Nations to deal with a multitude of issues and find solutions to problems ranging from preservation of international peace and security to promoting sustainable economic development, to poverty and disease eradication, and to peacebuilding and the promotion of human rights. There is a lack of financial resources to meet the demand for global expansion. The vast responsibilities that member nations entrust the United Nations is increasing. In addition to the need for economic reform, the United Nations needs to uphold its political reputation. It has been the subject of a great deal of criticism and attacks regarding its character as an organization. The United Nations has been stigmatized by many scandals that have affected the organization's reputation and credibility. The oil for food scandal and the multiple reports of sexual or financial misconduct on behalf of United Nations personnel in peace-keeping operations and at headquarters put the United Nations in a defensive position. These scandals raised concerns not only about the ability of the UN to sustain and deliver its services but also set to question its role in the future. As the UN navigates through media campaigns and memberships call for accountability and better management, the United Nations has to defend its position. It aims to restore its credibility and role, which has to address all aspects of the organization work, including issues such as accountability, responsibility, oversight, internal controls, and delegation of authority.

All in all, five out of many conferences, such as environment, women's rights, population control, a weapons ban, and terrorism, demonstrate that the United Nations is a proactive and effective global organization for international politics. The United Nations is committed to improve International relations, making it an effective global organization. On the other hand, the problems that the United Nations encounters include biotechnology, the Iraqi conflict, and the United Nations administration, which can get improved through proactive management with the help of the United Nations Council. These changes are necessary when the United Nations is committed to promoting international relations by covering the full range of human institution for the support of global progress, making it an effective organization in international relations.

Social Religion

The study of sociology toward religion enlightened my perspective on the practice of religion by observational research. I can take a "subjective" study, "supernatural" religion, and provide an objective observation of both the physical the religious characteristics used in worship services

1. Now that you know what sociology of religion is, what did you already know when you started the course?

I didn't know much about sociology. I knew that sociology was the study of people. The first thing that came to mind was a sociopath, and I wanted to gain insight towards the course. I didn't know so much about the sociology of religion, but religion plays a big part in my life. I consider myself a very religious person, going to church on Sundays, and continually wanting to read the Bible to gain meaning and understanding how life was in biblical times. It is important to me to have a solid foundation in religion to be able to live life the way God intended it to be. New learning gets challenging for me to jump into a subject.

2. What was new to you? What had you not thought about before?

What was new to me was the idea that sociology and religion look at the principles of faith such as belief, rituals, and intuitions. I have had the opportunity to study Judaism, Islam, and Voodoo in an in-depth manner, which gave me a new perspective on how life is for others. In Judaism, I learned that a Bar Mitzvah or Bat Mitzvah gets held at the age of thirteen and that it showed a girl or a boy coming of age. I also learned that the Torah was a sacred document that took a long time to make. Also, I learned that in Judaism they only believe in the first five books of the Bible, which is referred to as the Torah to them. In Judaism, people are very ritualistic and have a certain way of doing things.

Another new religion to me is Islam. I learned that Abraham's son Ishmael had a big part in the religion of Islam. Muhammad had a wife named Khadija, who was extremely wealthy. Even though he had wealth, he still felt his life was meaningless. He took a retreat to a mountain, and the voice of God spoke to him, so he wrote the Koran. I learned the importance of the five pillars of Islam and how they integrate into the Islam faith.

Voodoo is also a new religion. Voodoo is attractive to lower income citizens of Africa, Haiti, and the Dominican Republic. I learned that in Voodoo they believe in many gods, and priests and priestesses, and ancestors whom also get worshipped. Voodoo originated back in the British colonialism, and they have five million followers today.

I learned the difference between a cult and a religion. In a cult, the group displays an unquestioning commitment to its leader. Questioning and doubt are discouraged, and even members get reprimanded within a cult. Cults believe in mind-altering practices. The leadership dictates how the group should act or feel. The group believes themselves to have exalted status.

I learned the sociological definition from Kurtz, who says, "religion is a unified system of beliefs and practices, relative to sacred things that are to say things set apart and forbidden, beliefs and practices which unite into one single moral community called a church all those who adhere to them." Religion then consists of the beliefs about the sacred practice and rituals and the community or social organization of people drawn together by religious tradition. Every religion has a system of beliefs about the world and what should be sacred. These beliefs are important because it shapes an individual's frame of reference. I also learned that ritual practices sustain social order. Kurtz said, "The beliefs of religious tradition never standalone either from one another or for the life of the Community." I am more aware of the differences between a cult and a religion.

3. What do you agree with?

I agree that the study of sociology is essential. It provides an outside observation of societal patterns. For example, African-Americans and the practices of the slavery, I am African American too. Slave owners provided insights toward that period in history. I was able to see that, even though slavery was very harsh. The slave owners presented the slaves with a new religion, which helped the slaves cope with their work. Sociology seeks to answer questions for an outlook and insight between slave and slave owners.

I like how sociology researches prayers from different religions and different denominations of religions. For example, we studied popular hymns with affluent denominations, and we also studied hymns in less affluent. We were able to extrapolate data from research of the prayers. Sociology provides insight into a society and its functions—Christianity, Hinduism and Buddhism.

I like how sociology compares and contrasts wedding ceremonies from Buddhism to Hinduism to Muslim. I think it's useful for individuals who are not religious and they want to choose a religion for themselves. It gave me a greater awareness of how the various religions perceive marriage as a sacred object. I learned that an individual should make intelligent choices when selecting a religion, One should play grab bag. Sociology teaches us how we can separate our religious beliefs to make more conscientious decisions.

4. What do you disagree with?

I disagree with sociology when it doesn't cover the divinity of religions.

Sociology doesn't cover divine relationships between man and deity. Sociology only covers the physical aspects of religions and not the spiritual aspects. I did not like the fact that sports get considered as a religion. I understand how sports have belief, ritual, and institution, or social aspects; however, I would not consider it a religion like Christianity, Islam, Hinduism, or Judaism. I think of Voodoo more as a religion than of sports. I believe that sociology gets too impersonal and uses people as data, but I am not sure how it can be used effectively to help and maintain society.

In conclusion, this study has been beneficial by showing me a variety of different religions that I need not research on my own. I appreciate all the knowledge and literature that was used to help me learn. It has given me a high awareness and cultural sensitivity for others who are practicing religions other than my own. I believe this should be a requirement for all degrees so that everyone can learn to respect and acknowledge others instead of stereotype media perceptions toward different religions. It was genuinely beneficial to me, and I am thankful for that.

Taught Tradition

For my first cultural event, I viewed an independent film based on the story of a family of dysfunction interwoven in the Mummers tradition. In this chapter, I will explain the history of the Mummers, remark and summarize the cultural message I received from the independent film, based on Mummer tradition.

Mummers are costumed entertainers who entertain to welcome the New Year. The first known Mummers origin began in the Middle East and Europe. The Mummers have passed their culture from generation to generation. The first known Mummers New Year event in Philadelphia, Pennsylvania, dates back to the late seventeenth century. The Mummers in Philadelphia are comparable to the Mardi Gras performers in New Orleans. By the 1870s, an unorganized neighborhood celebration became an area-wide parade. The city of Philadelphia organized and sponsored the first Mummers Parade on January 1, 1901.

Since 1901, Philadelphia Mummers today total more than ten thousand entertainers. Fancy, Comic, Fancy Brigade, and String Band are divisions for Mummers participation. Wives and friends once created fancy costumes with hefty price tags, but now they are being outsourced to costume designers. A sixty-four-piece Mummers suit today can cost between thirty and eighty thousand dollars.

Philadelphians recognize and identify with the Mummers tradition. Morals and ethics lace within the Mummers culture. Community commitment and peak performance steer the Mummers into each New Year.

Learning about the Mummers tradition opened my mind toward the organization. Having lived in Philadelphia suburbs most of my life, I accepted the Mummers. Watching the independent film at Villanova University influenced my interest. The film showed the guts of the organization. However, more importantly, the film depicted a family struggling with marriage and divorce. I can identify with the family. I am also from a broken home. But the family makes the film more interesting because they have roots in the Mummers culture. The father in the story owned the Mummers club. The son participated in the string band division. The daughter helped the club wherever and whenever she could. The mother worked and struggled with her marriage.

The film portrayed every instance of a family struggle inside of a larger community. The point of the film attempted to grasp turmoil and confusion together within a huge culture. The Mummer club lacked satisfactory performance. This particular Mummers club wanted to improve its club results. At the same time, the family severely struggled with marriage. I remember when I was in high school struggling with my comfort and my identity. I noticed similar characteristics within the son and the daughter. Divorce is a significant issue, especially when children are involved.

I was delighted with the children's attitudes toward their family. I noticed initiative within the son and daughter. The family entirely stopped functioning, but the children were the final bond that held the family in little togetherness. Having divorced parents separates the home. Family unity deteriorates as well as relational health. Unhealthy emotions surface, along with stress breaking down the soul. I began to see this in the film.

Mummers are important. I do find irony in the film. I noticed the film has a strong Mummer tradition and a critical influence on individual family morals and ethics. For a culture to be so old and historical, Mummer tradition should make family character virtuous.

All in all, I thought the film was necessary. I learned a lot about tradition and family. When I watch the Mummers open the New Year, I will be pleased with their hard work. Mummer tradition should have recognition for the morals and the values they teach.

Civil Foundations

According to Marcus Tullius Cicero, "What can be grander or nobler than jurisprudence?"

The English dictionary states that law "is the principles and regulations established in a community by some authority and applicable to its people, whether in the form of legislation or of custom and policies recognized and enforced by judicial decision. Also, the English dictionary also states that any written or positive rule or collection of rules prescribed under the authority of the state or nation, for the people in its constitution." I intend to compare and relate principles of Nicomachean Ethics written by Aristotle to the investigation of Marcus Tullius Cicero on the laws. I will also contrast principles of vice according to Nicomachean ethics that prohibit universal legislation and of civil law according to Marcus Tullius Cicero's investigation on the importance of law.

Marcus Tullius Cicero wrote on the laws that provide an opinion toward politicians when conversing with Atticus. He proclaims that "not that I think that those who adopt this profession are altogether ignorant of the principles of universal legislation; but they are far more attentive to the civil law, which gives them a hold on the interest of the people." Marcus provides a statement toward the character of political figures during this period. Marcus questions the character of civil servants. Nicomachean Ethics by Aristotle begins with "Every art and every inquiry, and similarly, every action and pursuit is thought to aim at some good." Both Cicero and Aristotle are developing reasons for human behavior that influences human action for the good of the people. The accountable character becomes appropriate when good and virtuous action aims at some good. I believe Cicero meant that political figures need virtue to keep with the interest of the people.

Cicero provides another point. He declares that "the great moral law of nature, the practice of the civil law can occupy but an insignificant and subordinate station. We shall have to explain the true nature of moral justice, which is suitable and correspondent with the true nature of man. Last, of all, shall we have to speak of those laws and customs which get framed for the use and convenience of particular peoples, which regulate the civic and municipal affairs of the citizens, and which are known by the title of civil law." The character of political figures is important because the development of virtuous politicians determines the results of civic affairs. Virtuous decision-making is important and must be important for the good and the chief good of citizens. Aristotle supports this in Nicomachean Ethics by declaring that character of virtue "is by doing just acts that the just man is produced and by doing temperate acts the temperate man; without doing these no one would have the prospect of becoming good." Political figures are at their best when moral justice that governs citizens are moral in action and virtuous in character. Cicero writes "I wish to avail myself of authorities on the present occasion because as you see, the main object of this whole discussion is to strengthen the foundations of our Commonwealth, to establish its forces, and to benefit its population in all their relations… This then as it appears to me, hath been the decision of the wisest philosophers; that law, was neither excogitated by the genius of men, nor is it anything discovered in the progress of society; but a certain eternal principle, which governs the entire universe; wisely commanding what is right, and prohibiting what is wrong. Therefore, that original and supreme law is the Spirit of God himself; enjoying virtue, and restraining vice." Both Aristotle and he described the importance of virtue. Aristotle teaches how to establish and achieve virtue. Virtue creates just actions, and just actions create a just man. Virtuous politicians are a necessity to the welfare of citizenship because they are the ruling authority for citizen activity. In relative support to Cicero, Aristotle proclaims in Nicomachean Ethics that "I mean moral virtue; for it is this that is concerned with passions and actions, and in these, there is excess, defect and the intermediate. To feel passions and actions at the right times, concerning the proper objects, towards the right people, with the right motive, and in the right way, is what is both intermediate and best, and this is a characteristic of virtue…while the intermediate is praised and is a form of success and being praised and being successful are both aspects of virtue. Therefore, virtue is a kind of mean, since, as we have seen, it aims at what is intermediate." Virtue is easy to achieve. Aristotle provides another comment by stating that "For which reason also one is easy and the other difficult. To miss the mark is easy but to hit the target is difficult." The perfection of political character builds a foundation for citizens to achieve better happiness and satisfaction with civil life fundamentally.

However, the failure to achieve good character in a politician results in the breakdown of citizenship according to Nicomachean Ethics as written by Aristotle and in contrast to the investigation of Cicero's opinion on the importance of law. Aristotle writes about wrong actions and the consequences of inappropriate activity. The inappropriate response becomes significant when elected politicians lack moral and ethical control. Aristotle writes "But every action nor every passion admits of a mean; for some have names that already imply badness. For example, spite, shamelessness, envy, adultery, theft, and murder. For all of these things imply their names that they are themselves bad and no the excesses or deficiencies of them. It is not possible, then, to ever be right about them, one must always be wrong." America notices examples of this in our contemporary political figures. The quality of leadership has deteriorated as the time has passed.

In contrast, Cicero writes, "For every law which deserves the name of a law ought to be morally good and laudable, as we might demonstrate by the following arguments. It is clear that laws were originally made for the security of the people, for the preservation of cities, for the peace and benefit of society. Doubtless, the first legislators persuaded the people that they would write and publish such laws only as should conduce to the general morality and happiness if they would receive and obey them." In contrast, citizens cannot positively progress with leadership due to deficiencies in character. Virtue is hard to achieve, but the lack of virtue more natural kept can be dangerous. Political figures must be accountable at all times, or the state will experience demise.

I compared and contrasted Cicero's insights on the laws with Aristotle's Nicomachean Ethics. The virtue of law and character is both expressed by Cicero and Aristotle. The public character is a virtue that must be perfected in political office. However, the deficiency of moral and ethical character by way of virtue can tear and destroy civilization. To compare and contrast civil law from Cicero and Aristotle's Nicomachean Ethics by both the positive and the negative factors, explains and produces results from grand and noble jurisprudence that irrefutably sustain great civilizations.

Visitation

M y wife Marissa Bush invited me to attend a master's student event at Penn State Great Valley. The event was held on a Wednesday, April 6, 2010, and was intended to stimulate growth for the Penn State masters programs. The official title of the event was "Bring Your Friend to School Day." Penn State offers a variety of masters programs that students typically enjoy, but more specifically I had the opportunity to investigate the leadership program wherein my wife is a member.

The event began with a meet-and-greet in the reception area. Pizza and soda were served to open up the evening. In the first phase of the event, I was able to discuss a master's program that I sought interest. I found a program that taught the dynamics and the procedures of entrepreneurial businesses. Shortly after that, I found myself in a classroom setting where my wife began to introduce me to her colleagues and professor. Penn State Great Valley is a very prestigious university and has a beautiful campus. I felt comfort knowing that the school had accommodated me. The class knew that I went to Villanova for undergrad, and I was rather pleased with their open acceptance.

The lecture lasted for three hours. The professor discussed the principles of leadership. I had a tough time following the concepts. I was easily able to distinguish that their science of laws was not solely based upon Christ but the social mechanism of hierarchal science; therefore, I tried my best to follow along. Now that I look back on my past learning from University schools, especially from Penn State Great Valley, must have been and is very challenging. My knowledge rooted in Christ makes for a well-rounded education. I thought too going to Penn State would help me feel better. But having some time to reflect upon my experience at Penn State did not determine my collegiate career path.

I had a great time participating in the group activity held during the lecture. I had a great time watching the professor teach in poetic prose. I had a great time sharing in the tradition of Penn State. I think I had a tough time relating to the class within social science. Bless the people who attend Penn State Great Valley because I know that I would have a difficult time accepting the lack of God in its core principles. The students are very friendly, kind, and passionate about their learning, and I think that those virtues stand for something.

Overall, however, I did have a revitalizing experience. I had a great time learning about relativism at Penn State Great Valley. I think it is an excellent school for those who are technical-based and robust in personal attitudes. I want to thank my wife, Marissa, for opening my eyes to my first master's level class experience ever.

Greek vs. Bible

I will compare and contrast Nicomachean Ethics, the New Testament, Marcus Tullius Cicero, and the Old Testament to show similarities and differences between the Greek text and Hebrew text.

In my first comparison between Nicomachean Ethics and the New Testament, the chief good written from Nicomachean ethics has a similar message to the New Testament's "I am the world." Nicomachean Ethics writes that "Every art and every inquiry, and similarly every action an pursuit, is thought to aim at some good…Shall we not like archers who have a mark to aim to be more likely to hit upon what is right…but the chief good is evidentially something final." In the New Testament from the Gospel of John, Jesus spoke to his disciples and wrote, "I am the light of the world. Whoever follows me will never walk in darkness but will have the light of life." The messages are similar because Aristotle writes that the chief good is something special and something unique. Jesus personifies the chief good written about in Nicomachean Ethics. Aristotle says that "every action and pursuit is thought to aim at some good." Jesus's recommendation demonstrates the reason how to achieve the chief good, which is by "whoever follows me will never walk in darkness but will have the light of life."

To contrast Nicomachean Ethics and the New Testament, Aristotle writes on happiness and says that "We always choose for self and never for the sake of something else but honor, pleasure, reason, and every virtue we choose indeed for virtue themselves, but we choose them also for the sake of happiness judging that means of them we shall be happy." I find an opposite meaning in the Hebrew text of the New Testament where the Gospel of Luke states, "Blessed are you who are poor, for yours is the kingdom of God. Blessed you who are hunger now, for you will be filled. Blessed are you who weep now for you will laugh. Blessed are you when people hate you, and one day exclude you, revile you, and defame you on account of the Son of Man." It seems as though Aristotle is telling his followers that they must decide to be happy, and then they become happy. However, in the Gospel of Luke, Jesus is telling his disciples that no matter what state they are in they will inherit the happiness from God. Unlike Aristotle's teachings, Jesus is saying that selfless desires, in the end, achieve the kingdom of heaven a lot faster than pleasurable earthly desires that Aristotle writes. The text is essential because Aristotle's form of happiness lacks God's goodwill versus the Gospel of Luke's version stating that joy gets inherited through the kingdom of God.

To continue to compare the Greek text and Hebrew text, I have selected Marcus Tullius Cicero's work on laws in comparison and contrast to the Old Testament. The subtle difference between the two texts is the idea that God is unknown in the Greek text and is known in the Hebrew text. Cicero writes, "Since you grant me the existence of God and the superintendents of providence I maintain that he has been especially kind to man. This human precedent intelligent, complex, acute, full of memory, reason, and counsel which we call the supreme God generates a man in a more transcendent condition than most of his fellow preachers. For he is the only creature among the mortal races of animated beings and endued with superior reason and thought in which the rest are deficient when man's reason becomes right and perfect is justly termed wisdom." In the old Hebrew text of the Old Testament, I will compare the message written to Moses that states, "Then Moses went up to God; the Lord called to him from the mountain saying Thus you shall say to the house of Jacob and tell the Israelites you have seen what I have done to the Egyptians…If you obey my voice and keep my covenant, you shall be my treasured possession out of all my people. The whole earth is mine, but you shall be for me a priestly kingdom and a holy nation." Cicero's words to Atticus talk about bearing a responsibility to govern and control relationships between citizens of law and citizens under the law. Cicero is petitioning that it is in the most excellent condition being under God that a man can lead his people wisely. God's words to Moses are relative to Cicero's words to Atticus. God's message to Moses first of all was a direct relationship from divine to human. Secondly, God's message to Moses relinquished authority because Moses needed to have direction to govern the Israelites.

To contrast the two pieces, Quintus writes, "Now if nature hath given us law she hath also given us justice, bestowed reason on all she has equally bestowed the sense of justice on all and therefore did Socrates deservedly execrate the man who first drew a distinction in the law of morals for he justly conceived this error is the source of most human vices." On the other hand, Moses received a message from God stating that "You have seen for yourselves that I spoke with you from heaven. You shall not make Gods of silver alongside me. Nor shall you make for yourselves Gods of gold. You need to make for me only an altar of earth and sacrifice on it your burnt offerings and your offerings of well-being, your sheep and your oxen; in every place where I cause my name to will become remembered. I will come to you and bless you." Cicero describes the civil law as the law of man's wisdom that gets taken from nature. Unlike Moses, his civil law is a direct relationship from God to Moses. Cicero proclaims that man is a supreme being affected by nature's law. Unlike Moses, Cicero did not have a direct relationship with God to man.

In conclusion, the Greek text and the Hebrew text can get compared and contrasted. I explained various points for both in comparison and contrast for Greek and Hebrew text. The relationship between God and man is dynamic and structural to aid in the growth of human society.

Value in Life

Regarding your reading the introduction, foreword, and chapter one of the book *Inspiring Leadership: Character and Ethics Matter*, list those values that are most important in your life. In doing so, define ethics and character in your own words and describe your worldview and how it affects your overall behavior?

The most important values in my life are the military, education system, and family. I received the opportunity to serve in the United States Airforce, and it has shaped my worldview. I have always believed in the education system. I think education is vital for growth and stability in one's life. It provides the opportunity for individuals to grow and to develop and to be able to "give back" to society. I value my family immensely because of my family heritage. Being able to talk to every member on a regular basis keeps me in line with the past, present, and future. These are the values that I plan on instilling in my children.

My definition of ethics rests upon a global civilization with national competition on resources. One needs to maintain integrity for planetary survival. My interpretation of the character is a change in behavior over time toward global political issues that affect the lives of families to gather experience by working toward God's best interest for his people and his universe. My values, ethics, and character have influenced my overall behavior because it creates my actions that in good faith I intend to provide excellence, service through God, and integrity for my family and my country. Regarding your reading of chapter three of the book, *Inspiring Leadership: Character and Ethics Matter*, which public figures do you believe are truthful? How do they demonstrate their honesty?

I believe Barak Obama is truthful. He is a man of integrity. He designed a universal health care bill that became signed, June 2014.

President Barack Obama provided us with a stimulus package to re-condition the United States economy. He provided economic incentives for individuals and businesses that he campaigned for in 2008. Barack Obama has remained truthful from the first time he contested from the Senate to present in the office. Barack Obama notably has earned himself the Noble Peace Prize for his work with Iran and the Muslim population for nuclear disarmament and peace talks with the Eastern Muslim community. Barak Obama demonstrated consistency since his inauguration in 2008. He shows honesty, integrity, service to his country and excellence in what he does.

Broken Leadership

The purpose of this *chapter* is to explain a personal dilemma that fits into one of the four ethical paradigms listed in chapters one, four, and five of *How Good People Make Tough Choices* by Rushworth M. Kidder. I experienced a tough moral dilemma that nearly terminated my Job. Back in 2007, I worked for a company fresh from a technical school having only graduated in 2005; I began my career in drafting. I had some college experience but not enough to capture an architectural seat. I made do with drafting experience. My starting salary equaled to thirty-five thousand dollars a year. My first highest paying wage I have ever earned by the age of twenty-four. I worked hard to become a professional. Reflecting upon my experiences with the firm has enabled me to close a bad wound I fought with for three years.

My ethical dilemma began one year into my career. I thought I built relationships of truth and honesty that I learned from military experience. In conclusion of my career, I left with distrust and disappointment. I worked under the supervision of senior management who I have utmost respect and attention. The owners of the company provided direction for me to follow all directives under senior supervision. Throughout the time, I began to build a relationship with my superiors. We traded stories, smoked cigarettes together, participated in field exercises, and discussed future business plans. In the very beginning, I was told that the company had a high employee turnover. With a place I thought was great, how could the company have such a high turnover rate?

One morning, I was told by management that they needed details for a former employee. We were the only two people in the building that morning. I had happened to have my flash drive handy for a school that day. Management told me that he did not know how to download the document from the machine and asked if I could do it for management.

Well, to make a long story short, I did download those documents without the company's authorization, but in my defense, I also explained to him that I thought copying records from the machine was stealing. Management tried to persuade me that copying files from the computer was ethical and moral. To this day, I do not know who else knows about that incident, but I wish that I had moral and ethical support far superior to what I was asked to do.

After reading chapters one and four of Kidder's book, I know that I have experienced the truth versus loyalty paradigm. Kidder wrote, "Truth versus loyalty can be seen as honesty or integrity versus commitment, responsibility, or promise-keeping…the clash of core values support the idea that decision making becomes challenging for good people to make tough decisions." I experienced a truth versus loyalty dilemma. Not only was my integrity attacked, but my faith was also called upon for allegiance of unknown loyalty. Having less experience with ethics, I believed I had to make a tough decision with the time I was given. At least, I was able to defend myself by explaining to him that he was stealing.

After reading Kidder, I believed that management supported rule-based thinking. Kidder states that rule-based reasoning gets best explained as "Follow only the principle that you want everyone else to follow." Intentionally or not, I believed management subscribed to this approach. I do not want to place blame on them; however, I want them to become ethically aware of their environment and the lives of their followers. They had been put in a position of power and authority and did not act in a just and fair way. Not only for the company but also to themselves and me. As for me, I have prayed and repented for my sins.

I am addressing this ethical dilemma as a moral problem because I am sure that several companies experience issues such as integrity breach due to employee incompetence. Many companies—including my own, Worley & Bush Company—need to educate employers and employees about property protection. I would not want my information to become stolen. Even for those who do not own a company, identity theft has been an issue with doctors, lawyers, accountants, business owners, etc. I wish I could relive my actions to make better decisions. I have faith and good will that God will now lead my time morally.

Ethics and Leadership

I will discuss Kouzes & Posner's book *Credibility* with an agreement and critique relationship to Kidder's *How Good People Make Tough Choices* and Fisher & Martini's *Inspiring Leadership: Character and Ethics Matter*.

I will prepare two agreements and one critique based upon selected chapters from each text. I will provide an agreement reflection from chapters "Leadership is a Relationship" (Kouzes & Posner) about "Right versus wrong; why Ethics happens" (Kidder). I will solely provide an agreement reflection from the chapter "Credibility Makes a Difference" (Kouzes and Posner). Also, I will solely provide a critique on "Appreciating Constituents and Their Diversity." I intend to demonstrate a response to Kouzes & Posner's *Credibility* and Kidder's *How Good People Make Tough Choices*.

I agree with the text from chapters "Leadership Is a Relationship" and "Right versus wrong; why Ethics happens." I have found a relationship between the two texts. Kouzes & Posner state that, "Leadership is intangible. It is a performing art. It is an encounter. Leadership is something we experience in an interaction with another human being. Leadership is high in labor content. Leadership gets performed in many ways. Performance varies from leader to leader, from a constituent to constituent, and from day to day. No two leaders, no two constituent groups, and no two days in the life of a leader and constituents are exactly alike. Leadership acts by producing behaviors and the reception of those acts are inseparable. Constituents most often experience their needs becoming et or not met at the moment of the encounter." Furthermore, Kidder makes a point about the importance of ethics. Uneducated leaders emerge every day, but great leaders incorporate ethical policies or creeds that they follow. I believe Kidder provides insight into why and how great leaders culminate character to be considered more prepared, aware, and responsive than uneducated leaders. Kidder writes about three foundational ethical wrongs great leaders foster awareness. The first states that "It is wrong to pass a stopped school bus, take a candy bar without paying the shopkeeper, cut trees on your neighbor's property, or fail to curb your dog. More significant it is wrong to bribe public officials, refuse to pay rent, pass bad checks, or beat your spouse. These kinds of wrongdoing involve failures of compliance with clearly specified laws. Lack of compliance can arise ignorantly or intentionally-either because we do not know the law and law applications, or because we willfully choose to violate the law." The second ethical wrong Kidder introduces is "We also use wrong to describe that which does not accord with the facts generally known… calling in sick when you are not, asserting that the gunk in the river is not from your factory when it is, or claiming that, as president, you did not know about Watergate when you did. These sorts of "wrongs" lie at the core of the legal process, where a great deal of energy is spent trying to determine the relationship between stories the parties say happened and the truth that happened." The third evaluation of ethical wrong Kidder introduces starts with, "Suppose I see someone shoplifting, but I say nothing to the supermarket manager. Suppose I do not get around to feeding my dog today. Suppose I promise to meet you at noon, but decide to lunch with someone else and do not bother to call you. If we have even the most rudimentary concept of duty, we will probably see these lapses in ethics." The point I intend to make describes the education of a great leader. Taken from *Credibility*, a leader interacts to create an experience with another human being. Infusing principles adopted from *How Good People make Tough Decisions*, violating the law; departing from the truth, and deviating from moral rectitude begin to mold characteristics of a great leader.

I also agree with the text from Kouzes & Posner's chapter, "Credibility Makes a Difference." Once a leader establishes credibility, he/she must maintain it. Kouzes & Posner describe six practices that allow a leader to carry trust in his/her credibility. I will cite a description for six practices and will reflect upon credibility. *Credibility* discusses six principles: discovering yourself, appreciating constituents, affirming shared values, developing capacity, serving a purpose, and sustaining hope. "Discovering yourself begins with the enhancement of credibility by the exploration of the inner territory. To be a credible leader, you must clarify your values and the standards by which you choose to live your life." The second principle—appreciating constituents—described as "To be a leader, you must also develop a deep understanding of the collective values and desires of your constituents." Principle three—affirming shared values—states that "Credible leaders honor the diversity of their many constituencies. They also find common ground for agreement on which everyone can stand." Principle four—developing capacity—states that "People cannot contribute to the aims and aspiration of an organization if they do not know what to do and they cannot help if they do not know how to do it." Principle five—serving a purpose—states that "Leadership is a service. Leaders serve a purpose for the people who have made it possible for them to lead their constituents." The last principle introduces the idea of sustaining hope, which states that "Credible leaders keep hope alive. An upbeat attitude is essential in these troubling times of transition." The main idea of *Credibility* intends to deliver the idea that all fundamental leaders need a plan or roadmap. While on the journey, everyone should get along and enjoy the trip. Be thankful and courteous of one other. Create a pleasant environment and atmosphere to develop the experience. Then peacefully go home after the itinerary is complete. The six principles are the roadmap a developing leader should incorporate.

I will provide a sole critique of *Credibility* from the chapter "Appreciating Constituents and Their Diversity." According to the book, Posner writes, "The workplace of the twenty-first-century demands appreciating diversity, not simply tolerating it, managing it, or even being able to create a "melting pot." Such homogeneity is no longer feasible today. Organizations themselves are also becoming more diverse. Diversity does, however, make leaders' job more complicated. With the greater resources, talents, and energy come new challenges and alternatives. Problems occur every day, and a leader must take action on every issue. After all, constituent interaction with a leader creates an experience. How effective are these leaders on elimination issues such as racism, sexism, and abortion? The job market speaks highly about workforce diversity, but the last question on the application asks: Have you been convicted of a felony? So where do these people go to find jobs in the workplace? *Credibility* speaks highly in favorable conditions, but what about conditions of threat and of war?

All in all, credibility and ethics provide qualities of character for a developing leader.

Weave together a definition, a foundation for ethics, a road map, direction guide, and a realistic worldview; an educated potential leader can be more prepared, aware, and responsive to his/her constituents and surrounding peers. I provided agreements and a critique reflection of Kouzes & Posner's book *Credibility*, along with a referenced source from Kidder's *How Good People Make Tough Choices*. Overall, I will be able to use these sources heavily in my future as a leader.

Risk & Business

Notification for American investors, such as myself, to increase awareness of sovereign risk before authorizing the purchase of Ghana's government securities to use investor strategies—for example, dollar cost averaging to build returns from Ghana's nation-state sovereignty. I will identify three risks that will be cultural, financial, and political barriers that indicate risks to American investors.

Ghana's constitutional democracy has provided social protection mechanisms for social assistance and capacity. Social protection is a form of government control to improve the lives of indigent individuals, households, and communities (2006). A little less than half of the population of Ghana is considered poor (40 percent), which in turn means that the citizens have trouble providing for themselves and their families. These conditions pose a considerable risk for American investors because many times people do not have the authorization to access important resources for long-term cultivation. This data is vital for American investors since stability stems from access to as many or all resources as they need, both natural and human-made. Large amounts of capital spending influence American markets and culture. The location of undiscovered resources found in poor communities presents a sovereign risk factor. Capital crime, theft, and disruption impede economic and social production. Slow government response to support a needy population indicates a weak government. Forty percent of Ghana's population is poor; poverty in Ghana creates tension between citizens causing the country to experience friction and a strong economic divide. The GNI per capita in 2008 is $670. 30 percent of Ghana's population is underneath the international poverty line, which amounts to $1.25 per day. On average, this demonstrates slow economic growths. It was a good start for Ghana, but American investors identify

Ghana as an undeveloped country and a target for high sovereign risk. The total adult literacy rate of 65 percent shows that the government has not taken an aggressive role in education to increase participation in global politics and global economics for the country of Ghana.

Improper sanitation processes prohibit and discourage clean trade. American investors frown upon unhealthy lifestyle choices by the government and the lack of individual development. Pandemic diseases such as HIV/AIDS and malaria deter trade with Ghana from a socio-economic point of view. Unsanitary health practices create risks that American investors shun.

Telecommunication, scarcity portrays Ghana's population to lack quick communication. Thirty-two out of one hundred people own a telephone. American investors need instant communications to meet the demand of the community. Only four out of one hundred are Internet users who spend through a borderless economy. That ratio is unattractive to American investors because international trade is minimal. There has been a decline in population growth from 1990 to 2008 by .5 percent. A declining population rate indicates a lack of internal medicine, which illuminates the difference in government focus. Life expectancy of Ghana in 2008 has increased to fifty-seven years of age (UNICEF—Ghana, 2010), but the United States' life expectancy amounts to 77.9 years. This datum suggests Ghana has an undeveloped healthcare system that lacks internal medicine for its population sovereignty. Ghana is a sovereign risk to American investors because longevity in Ghanaian workforce creates inconsistent returns.

Ghana's inflation rate continues to increase as well as their poverty level, showing a lack of success in its government sovereignty. The average annual inflation rate is 24 percent. American investors would have to provide more cash for the same product, very unattractive. Inflation indicates a lack in Ghana's industrial production in comparison to international powerhouses. Ghana illustrates a concern for investor monies. Slow production and high costs show high volatility in Ghana's economic system.

Of Ghana's population, 47 percent believe in domestic violence. Ghana presents a sovereign risk, which feeds into Ghana's lack of economic production. Inadequate and obsolete healthcare practices in Ghanaian history determine the treatment capacity to release persons of domestic violence back into the workforce. Slipshod humanitarian efforts tie into Ghana's central government general competitive spending budget because of 7 percent of its budget funds healthcare (UNICEF—Ghana, 2010). This figure is shallow compared to that of the United States' at 25 percent to improve encompassing changes to respecting systems (UNICEF— the United States, 2010).

For American investors to invest in this country, this barriers will have to be addressed by the central government. America has yet to provide services and products in the Ghanaian region. Production in Ghana consists of countries such as Britain and China and not the United States. All in all, an American investor's focus on social, financial, and political sovereignty risks impedes and prohibits successful trade negotiations with American investors.

Borderless Economy

There are four factors that impact future students of a borderless economy to help minimize risks and uncertainties involved with the creation of the Internet technology and data sharing. Government, language, curriculum, and employment opportunities are areas where I focused my attention on as solutions to minimize uneducated directions in a borderless economy. A borderless economy contains many variables that make any novice unfruitful. The goal to create a borderless economy more effective is determined by a system of beliefs put into education year after year to stabilize and build a digital outline.

Students in public schools need to be prepared for a borderless economy. In government, schools need to teach international laws and organizations. They need to take an expansionist point of view instead of isolationism on world politics. World politics needs to be inclusive managing differences between all nations and needs to accept ethnic-religious government backgrounds. The goal should be to welcome a borderless trade to prevent harmful or illegal activity such as the black market.

There should be a universal business language accepted by nations to help with uniformity. This universal language would help elevate miscommunications between business parties. Students should be able to attend any university in a cosmopolitan ideology. Vocabulary does not have the same meaning, but it should. The history of language should get included in the public school curriculum to give students a necessary understanding of global interaction.

Teachers and administrators should work collaboratively with other nations to develop curriculum standards that would be universal to guide students in a borderless economy. A curriculum is a guideline that will prepare students to interact and perform with other nations for global instruction on the borderless economy. It should incorporate ethics policies to guide business practices in communities worldwide. Teachers should explore topics in greater detail such as the economics of different countries. They also should look into organizations that support borderless economies such as the World Trade Organization. Public school students can be more knowledgeable of employment opportunities in a global economy. New technology and data processing positions can have an opening in one country and have an employee in another location (state). Twenty-four-hour work service becomes available with the borderless economy. Public school students can learn how to work on a twenty-four-hour clock to maximize their efforts and time independent of location. In some ways, students can learn to become their bosses, save money, and minimize time spent working for resources in a borderless economy.

The four suggestions of government, language, curriculum, and employment opportunities amount to partial solutions to solve uncertainties of a borderless economy. The greater awareness that students foster for a borderless economy will produce a more productive and lucrative economy for individualistic success. All in all, students can learn how to implement policies to make for a clean and friendly economy.

Company Development

I read Chapters one to four in *The Talent Masters* book. The book was excellent and influential for me. I learned new vocabulary like *business acumen* and *meritocracy*. I learned that to develop talent; I need to "spot, find, and develop people through predictable, consistent, repetitive processes to develop candor and trust." I am learning to build intimacy within an organization built on the "core values of a person's behaviors, beliefs, and talents." This development process is used to understand "cause, context to create timely growth and development." I thought the principles of *The Talent Masters* were interesting. The first principle starts with "an enlightened leadership team." It states, "That a leader should be committed to creating a culture of talent mastery by personal involvement." I agree that a leadership should have personality because it builds a sense of organizational intimacy. The intimacy also reflects upon a leader's ability to engage others within the organization to create the culture.

Principle two talked about meritocracy through differentiation. Many companies merit their employees. I think merit through differentiation develops individual talent to separate roles within an organization. After reading the term *meritocracy*, I thought this is a word that I have never heard. I have heard of systems based on merit, but when you put the word in perspective, such as *meritocracy*, it opens up the understanding that a person gets judged on their responsibilities, talents, and credentials.

Principle three talks about working values. Old talent must teach a new skill. When I think of this system, it reminds me of a fraternity or sorority, or even more prominent, the United States presidency. Traditions and values must be passed along to new talent, or the culture will not remain subsistent. The fourth principle states, "An organization must have a culture of trust and openness." A successful organization develops its people built on accurate information regarding strengths, development needs, and candid ability. Many organizations today lack this principle creating new work for responsible leaders. Global markets call for quick actions and repetitive processes.

Principle five talks about the rigorous talent assessment. "Talent Masters have the same goals, results, and orientation in their people processes as they do in the financial systems." Talent analytics and metrics are a big business today. Small organizations will build talent if they introduce talent assessment. I think this is very integral today.

Principle six builds a business partnership with human resources. Human resource elements get held within the similar statuses of organizations chairpersons. I think every employee feels comfortable to develop trust in an organization based upon a department held in the best interest of its employees. I feel comfortable knowing that human resources have programs for employee development.

Principle seven establishes continuous learning and improvement. We live to learn and to develop an enrichment of lives and communities. Education stimulates open discussion to determine procedures for collaborative leadership. Leadership in the community taught by Professor Benjamin Schuster identifies the problem of leadership today. We need to take a collaborative approach to leadership. Educating communities locally to globally enriches and increases the quality of lives.

Leadership Concepts

The concept of leadership starts with an idea to manage differencess. Every leader, including myself, seeks counsel for "What do I have to do as a leader?" Every leader strives for success. A leader has the opportunity to lead anyone by example. It is important for me in a leadership position for others to achieve enrichment. A good leader is selfless. The leader incorporates a higher being into his/her message. In my social distinction, God influences my daily leadership messages. I learned that traditional leadership captures a moment to deliver results for market participants. Results are what drive people in leadership capacities. The goal is to help you with service and resources.

A leader introduces the participant only by invitation to an intended market with hopes of closing a deal.

For example, the CDC Valentine's Day dance is an example where I was invited to lead. During the day on Friday, the CDC (where I worked) held a Valentine's Day dance for the students. The first opportunity for leadership development occurred with the social selection. Every student sought social distinction. Student, instructors, and photographers gathered socially to celebrate Valentine's Day. Every student sought acceptance and social success. I taught the student I work with to enjoy with reverence, enrichment, and social satisfaction through intellect. We danced; we learned and built relationships for a central trust in each other.

Overall, a leader needs to seek counsel in a higher being, capture purpose, market, resources to deliver enriching results. Leadership is an essential aspect of peoples' lives. We strive to become leaders of our day. An author once said, "A leader is one who knows the way, goes the way and shows the way." This quote sums up the meaning of leadership.

Leadership with Character

A leader is a student first. He or she must attain education, own some business, whether it be a company or a farm. A leader must be held to the highest social reverence. He or she must practice religion, hold household, and participate in the community. As an example of duty, a leader also engages with volunteerism and charity. Great leaders are honored. I believe leadership attributes include education, employment, business or farm ownership, religious practice, have household and community participation. Once these qualities get met, a leader can begin their process to educate, mentor, consult, and then lead. My leadership starts with my ethnicity. I am an African American male. African American males are more likely to be found in the penal system and on government aid, lacking healthcare, education, and financial stability.

African American males are less likely to hold household, employment, practice religion, and participate in the community, much less lead. The world began with education. Man learned about geography. The Bible states Adam and Eve were banished from Eden to live and work outside in unfamiliar territory. African Americans nevertheless Africans, relative to data today need leaders. Social conditions mentioned in the shared value journal can lead to Africans and African Americans helping to increase economic proficiency. In Africa more than the United States, companies who employ leaders can take a shared value approach to stimulate economic and social development. Leaders are engaged in improving societal issues such as natural resource, water usage, health and safety, work conditions, and equal treatment in the workplace. Leaders improve conditions by solving problems involving social conditions and communities. However, traditional business effects social activity instead of meshing with social action.

Leaders today mistake the big picture for economic proficiency. Twenty-first-century leaders solve social issues and problems in the community, connected to financial competence. I am an African American student learning the leadership program. My goal is to achieve a sustainable community within African American society. Action starts at the high school level. African American students need to seek to enrichment with the protection of intellectual property. Also, those who lived in impoverished communities need nonprofit involvement. Social work, household rehabilitation, and employment assistance need attention. My company, Worley & Bush Company, needs to work together with nonprofit organizations for support and resource. This joint venture creates a shared value the journal references. Programs like trash pickup for incentive in African American communities, tree planting, and environmental preservation can get conducted with supervision for African American adults who need to do community service. The aim is to achieve "a successful community, not only to create a demand for products but also to provide critical public assets and a supportive environment. A community needs successful businesses to provide jobs and wealth creation opportunities for its citizens," according to the journal. African American communities lack gainful economic and social support from businesses in African American communities.

Business School Application

My family and I own a Christian clothing company, the Worley & Bush Company. Our company retails stylish attire for men, women, and children. Learning business acumen will give Worley & Bush Company the competitive advantage. Business models are important today for companies that transition from good to great. As part of my Villanova Leadership Studies curriculum, I have learned that people are an important resource. However, I lack business logistics relationship to human resources. Strong faith in Jesus led me to Villanova University. I have an opportunity to participate in current studies based on secular views with a theological approach.

The Villanova School of Business teaches scientific principles with religious support and background. I started my academic career in Christian schools. I spent time learning academic instruction in public schools. My faith led me to Villanova and on to the School of Business. If I afford this opportunity not only will I be able to graduate? I will be able to transition into the workplace built on principles of morality, ethics, and virtue. I will work hard and try my best. I will maintain my faith and tradition. I will ask questions when I need further explanation. I will assist classmates, and I will participate. I have a business goal. I want to set a personal goal to achieve business competence and success within the Summer Business Institute. I am honored to be a candidate for the Summer Business Institute at Villanova University.

Violence and Justice in the World

According to Webster's dictionary, the definition of violence is an "exertion of physical force to injure or abuse." I have learned three forms of violence that can occur with just one individual or involve and impact even as many as a community. Violence comes in varying degrees of severity and impact on both individuals and communities.

The first type of violence discussed is *intraviolence*, which occurs within an individual who tries to harm themselves. Intraviolence can take the form of the physical, mental, social, and emotional turmoil of that person. People who abuse themselves take away any opportunity they may have to flourish in their community. One can harm him or herself in the physical form by damaging his or her body with self-inflicted wounds, cuts, and bruises. Another way one can harm himself or herself is by abusing drugs, alcohol, and the abuse of over-the-counter or prescription medications. From my understanding, one can commit to intraviolence by practicing malnutrition (anorexia or bulimia) when he or she has access to proper nutrition. Also, it is my understanding that mental abuse is another form of intraviolence. The overuse of profanity can contribute to intraviolence within individuals and the community. Stress and over-deprivation of one's body can cause an individual to suffer from intraviolence. There are people in our community who have barriers to health care, and this can also be a form of intraviolence. The lack of health care for those with mental illnesses can seem like such horrible outcomes when we live in such a prominent society.

There is another dimension of intraviolence, and it is called *social intra-violence*. My comprehension of social intraviolence is when an individual does not obey and practice rules within his or her society. Those who do not follow the laws and regulations set before them in turn separate themselves and are many times labeled as outcasts or troublemakers who can cause disorder in their community. Persons who suffer from social intraviolence find it challenging to function in situations that require some participation (usually public). I also think that persons who suffer from social intraviolence lose their purpose within an educational setting. Individuals post low scores on standardized test as well as lack of educational resources to compete in society. Many factors can impact one's life, and I also think that the emotional aspects of an individual can lead to intraviolence. Unfulfilling relationships can cause a breakdown in an individual. Individuals who do not accept differences with people in their communities and societies can lead to emotional distress and dissension.

The second form of violence discussed is called *interviolence*. This type of abuse occurs when exchanges happen from one individual to another. This form of violence can also involve similar effects on one's physical, mental, social, and emotional state. Typically, this form of violence can occur when inequality occurs between a person and individual, a person to family, a person to the group, or a person to a community. This form of violence occurs when there is a breakdown in communication between parties. The aggressor has the role of being insubordinate and usually gets punished in the community.

Interviolence frequently occurs in our society and to me is sometimes linked to communication challenges and respect issues. In our society, we are all overwhelmed by the use of technology that we have not learned how to communicate when difficult situations arise correctly. If people learned proper communication tactics, we would be able to find various solutions to the problems incurred. The other part is that younger and younger persons are not respecting elders, and this too causes emotional violence. Just recently, there was a news article about a caregiver who was misusing funds of a disabled adult. The violence occurred is a younger person taking advantage of a person's physical and mental state, therefore, creating interviolence.

The third form of violence is called structural violence. Structural violence is a sophisticated form of violence. From the reading, structural violence gets described as "invisible in complex social structures." Structural violence occurs when inequity is built into the political, legal, and economic structure of citizens who are disadvantaged. According to the reading also, structural injustice creates suffering and death. The lack of access to resources of a disadvantaged group causes political and social friction that leads to a revolution at its worst and dissension in the least. Everyone meaning, race, ethnicity, religion, participate in communities that suffer from inequity. When friction between those who have access to resources and those who do not increases, there's the likelihood that structural violence will occur.

When thinking about structural violence, it is reminiscent to the people who have barriers to resources that others many times take for granted. When you think about all the items we have at our fingertips, many members of our society do not have access to resources. We have to be mindful of these barriers to make sure that violence is not related to structural/systemic issues in society. I have learned three forms of violence that can occur with inequities from an individual leading up to a community. Intraviolence, interviolence, and structural violence are the three forms of violence. The greatest form of violence is structural violence and is due to built-in structures of societies that are invisible but can cause more inequity and disparity between persons, groups, and communities. Intraviolence and interviolence deal with personal injustice, such as physical, mental, emotional, and social differences. Violence relating to personal inequity is more likely to be eliminated within a group and a society. We as members of a community have an ethical and moral right to make sure we educate people around us of the forms of violence. If we can teach appropriately, communicate effectively, and respect each other, we will be able to reduce the varying degrees of violence that affect our society.

Christian Affairs

James Loney belongs to Christian peacemaker team. This organization was founded in 1988 by Mennonite to increase Christian non-violence resistance toward injustice. Each peacemaking team can get deployed at a moment's notice. James Loney was not successful during Operation Iraqi Freedom. His team was captured hijack at gunpoint. Christian peacemaker teams are nonviolent workers who aim to negotiate peace terms. James Loney, along with his peacemaking group, was held captive. Every risk they take may not be successful, but with the global movement, peacemaking will eventually turn popular opinion toward global politics.

Christian peacemakers are and non-government organizations that received help from the Red Cross and the United Nations. The Christian peacemakers have built a relationship with other non-government organizations to receive assistance for injustice and war in the global community. Christian peacemakers are stewards for nonviolent protest. They rally supporters and workers to carry out Christian faith directives.

Christian peacemakers believe that restorative justice resolves global conflict. In the case of Iraqi freedom, James Loney and men were held captive. Upon a rescue by British soldiers, James Loney and two others became liberated. This case has been an example of personal forgiveness that is symbolic of restorative justice. A press conference reported, Christian theme forgiveness and survival. The Christian peacemakers, who were held in Iraqi freedom, spoke of forgiveness to their captors.

Groups like the Christian peacemakers have built an identity to challenge retributive justice in exchange for restorative justice. I agree with their works. James Loney is important because he once was a victim of injustice. He can apply his experience to the restorative justice model. In wartime, peacemakers may be the personnel to resolve the conflict.

I agree with Loney's mission. I would not risk my own life to protest against violence and injustice. I became more interested in his hijacking experience. These men were held captive and survived the war. For someone to live through that experience and tell the story is honorable. I thought James Loney's story is symbolic for restorative justice, especially when the group did not seek retribution but instead offered forgiveness. I think this story is an example of God's forgiveness during wartime conflict. Christian values such as love, faith, and forgiveness are common themes of the Christian peacemakers and Christians worldwide. I agreed with James Loney's position when he said that sometimes hope is more important than success. I think victory is important to profit organizations. But the achievements for nonprofits collectively are concerned with measuring the number of people an organization can member. I do not agree that these men practice nonviolent peace agreements. I think someone in their party should carry a weapon like a soldier or security officer. I do not believe any lesser toward their nonviolent efforts.

This example taught the value of men and women who practice non-violent peace negotiating. Solving wartime conflict does not have to end with guns drawn but instead offer an alternative to ending the conflict. Peacemaking is a big business. Faith and love motivate the Christian peacemakers. The story of James Loney is an example of restorative justice.

A Scope In Marriage

I read an article about successful marriage by James V. Gau. He states that clients who ask want to know how many couples he has kept together. James believes it is his role to help each spouse understand their part in a relationship so that each may grow and change. He states even if only one spouse achieves personal growth, he still regards this as a successful marriage therapy because it is less likely that he or she will make the same mistakes in the next relationship.

James makes a connection between mothers and infants the same way that a husband correlates to his wife. His theory is about differentiation. He states, "Primordial relationship between mother and infant greatly affects one's ability to differentiate in life." To differentiate is being able to anticipate her infant's needs. James refers to a mother explicitly focusing on her infant. According to James, the first month of life requires a merger of mother and infant for the infant survival. When in conflict does differentiation begin? When a mother is secure enough to contain her infant's frustration, and she did not retaliate and experienced the mother as a separate individual.

The infant becomes a child and then adolescent. By this point, the adolescent develops subjectivity of personal experience. James makes a point that the adolescent feels free to experiment due to trust in a secure parent. The adolescent does not have to guess what his or her parents need or want to approve behaviors. James relates mother to child relationship as a process of differentiation that extends to a marital relationship.

James makes conclusive statements about relationships between spouses. "When the concerns and responsibilities of life impinge on a spouse, and the spouse fails to anticipate the needs of the other, the spouse is likely to reproach." The spouse is less likely to reach assurance after the conflict in action for spousal needs have occurred. James states the idea of a merger is important because he says that "At every merged relationship is the urgent, even desperate desire for one's spouse to meet one's needs. Not meeting the needs could be interpreted as abandonment or rejection." He believes that when a spouse is required to change, it adds to hostility and pressures a spouse that results in a distance and retaliation to survive in the relationship. When the blaming occurs in the relationship, it is due to the merger and lack of differentiation.

James states that differentiation is the process of learning to separate from and connect to a loved one. Anxiety in a spousal relationship can move to merger blindly in an approach to differentiation. James notes that early in life we create ways to protect ourselves. "We learn to act out, devalue and project ourselves or we learn to please, smile, and use humor." Anxiety, James states, comes from the unconscious and is typically reactionary, exaggerated, and generalized.

James mentions intimacy can also be a source of differentiation. Intimacy to James is bilateral. Intimacy is validating a spouse and reciprocal, mutual, and shared in beliefs. James states, "Intimacy is the process of learning to separate from and connect with a spouse." Differentiation fails when a spouse does not separate but withdraw.

James provides strategies to arrive at differentiation. The first idea is "learning to use our anxiety instead of it controlling the relationship." Anxiety looks at a conflict that sometimes makes a spouse withdraw. Learn the process of self-soothe will achieve differentiation. The second idea is to state our experience, feelings, thoughts, needs, and desires. It's the "what we can and cannot do" principle. The object of the game is to demonstrate self-control. The third idea is to be self-aware. As long as spouses can speak about themselves, they talk attractively and credibly. The fourth idea speaks about mirroring. This idea makes use of achieved sufficient differentiation so that spouses can focus on the other. The anticipate disagreement and can represent each spouse's point of view with accuracy. The results are that spouses can negotiate, accommodate, and be generous.

I have not heard of the term *differentiation* used in marriage. James links ideas about a mother-child relationship and applies it to marriage. Differentiation solves issues of motives for getting married according to chapter one of *Before the Wedding*. Differentiation can get applied to the ten reasons why people get married according to the book. I will refer the idea of differentiation in a couple of sentences to the motives of getting married explained in *Before the Wedding*.

1. *The need to feel adequate.* James theory of differentiation would be to briefly state our experiences, feelings, thoughts, needs, and desires and to maintain self-control and credibility.

2. *The need to avenge lost battles.* The differentiation theory strategy would be the third strategy. The plan calls for a spouse to be self-aware of thoughts, feelings, and desires. The focus is self-directed and authoritative. A spouse maintains credibility as a result.

3. *The need to get a personal needs met.* I think idea four can be applied here. A spouse would practice mirroring to focus on the other.

4. *The need to gain a parent for life.* I think the idea of differentiation as a whole concept starts with being able to trust a spouse and allow for exploring in subjectivity.

5. *The need to have sex.* I think the first strategy of differentiation can be applicable, managing anxiety and using it to control the conflict. A spouse can self-soothe and self-comfort.

6. *The need to become a parent.* I would say strategy number three of self-awareness would help this situation. Speaking about self-awareness empowers a spouse with credibility.

7. *The need to satisfy a love addiction.* Strategy three, to achieve differentiation, a spouse needs to have the self-awareness to achieve intimacy and vulnerability.

8. *The need to escape the drudgery of single life.* Strategy number one, using anxiety to self-soothe and self-comfort draws couples closer to differentiation.

9. *The need to continue a self-destructive life*. Strategy one in differentiation talks about managing anxiety. The ability to self-soothe, and self-comfort can be applied to stop self-destructive actions.

10. *The need to bring about a self-centered life plan*. Strategy number four talks about mirroring in differentiation strategies. A spouse can represent his or her spouse's point of view accurately and empathetically. They can negotiate, accommodate, and act generously.

Why Justice?

Justice gets explained as "the quality of being just; righteousness, equitableness, or moral rightness: to uphold the justice of a cause." My understanding of justice is similar to the definition of truth. To me, justice is action taken against a defender to restore original faith and trust in the victim. I believe when an offender gets punished for a crime, justice is the means to repair a relationship of equity for the offender. Justice can only occur with inequity between a victim and an offender. The real purpose behind justice is to seek fairness among all parties. Justice is a very subjective topic because it is almost always right in the eye of the beholder.

I could relate this to my life back in 2004 when I was still part of the United States Air Force, and I became sick. I eventually became diagnosed with a lifelong disability that I felt as if I was due justice. The Department of Veteran Affairs decided that on my behalf I would be able to become disabled and collect compensation. I honestly do not want to have a lifelong disability but have been compensated with justice, the fact knowing that the VA has upheld the right to continually offer me medical care, disability, and continuing support throughout my life.

I understand justice as a faculty of the criminal court system. Justice gets earned when a judge and jury punish a criminal. I do believe there are some criminal offenders out in the world that have yet to meet their justice for their crimes. Over the years, the USA justice system has progressively gotten more reputable. I do believe that criminals who have not been tried by the justice system have seemingly escaped justice. Justice does not necessarily have to be a criminal trial; however, it can be something as small as a dispute with your neighbor as long as fairness and rightness get achieved.

The first form of justice we have learned about is called retributive justice that is the current justice system of today's penal system. According to the text, there are five qualifications to meet the retributive justice. The five include "Guilt must be fixed, the guilty get what they deserve, offenders receive the infliction of pain, the process measures justice, and the breaking of the law defines the offense."

In today's society, it is apparent that we use the retributive justice model. We start with number five in each case to ensure when defining the outcomes of breaking laws are accurate and just. We align our processes to make sure we are following the law the way as written. Of course, there are many times when "nuances" and "discrimination" happen, in which case we adjust and refocus our model to offer justice in each situation. Our justice system is not perfect however we can try to strive to make each situation as accurate and just as we can.

The second form of justice is called the restorative justice. Restorative justice can function asynchronously with retributive justice. Restorative justice mainly means to restore a relationship between a victim and an offender. The importance relies upon the relationship between the victim and the offender. The book states, "Crime is a violation of people and relationships. It creates obligations to make things right. Justice involves the victim, the offender and the community in a search for solutions which promote repair, reconciliation, and reassurance." Truth searching is a great way, to sum up, the understanding of justice.

The readings and the discussions have increased my understanding of justice by creating a literal evaluation model of the justice system. I have learned that retributive justice is very harsh; however, our society currently works within this style. Justice is something that should get used across all aspects of our lives. It is a valuable lesson to teach our children and grandchildren. Too many times these days we lose sight of the true meaning of justice because of what the world tells us to believe. I think we could use decisive thinking when trying to figure out which type of justice would be the best based on the type of crime committed. Retributive justice is an autonomous system that does not help the relationship of the victim and offender but aims to alienate one from the other. I have learned that a restorative justice helps with closure between the victim and the offender relationship. Restorative justice, I think, could also be used to decrease criminal punishment with smaller sentencing, but more importantly, create a dialog between the victim, offender, and community. I think society functions better when all questions get answered by the offender. The community can evaluate the crime for better security, response, or function of the community so that everyone will be on the same page.

Popular Vote, Electoral Vote

The 2000 election did not damage the presidential election process; however, it did bring a large amount of press that even the election for president can present with glitches. The election process was not illegal about the constitution. The election process was a reminder that elections can introduce flaws just like anything else in society. The presidential campaigns for George Bush, Jr. and Al Gore resulted in a Republican win over Gore. The presidential election was a close race. The election came down to the electoral votes in Florida. Al Gore won the popular vote for the election, but George Bush, Jr. won the most electoral votes, granting him the US presidency. George Bush, Jr. won was because Florida had a voting recount that gave him a winner-take-all win for Florida in electoral votes.

The 2000 election gave awareness to American voters. Many did not want to see George Bush win. The popular vote for Al Gore was an indication that the American people wanted to see a Democratic president. The 2000 election was a wake-up call for US citizens. It does cause concern in my eyes, as it almost seems like it *had* to happen that way to ensure George Bush a win. The election process, I believe, is seen as damaged in the eyes of some; however, in every job, there are "damages." Not every situation is perfect, and there is always room for error, but it makes you think harder.

The election demonstrated that Gore could win the poll but still lose the election. It can be quite confusing to citizens how the actual electoral votes get distributed; however, it is consistent with history in that every election follows the same process.

I agree with the Electoral College process. George Bush, Jr. won fair and square. He won 271 electoral votes. The presidency could have swayed in the other direction pointing to Gore if he won the Twenty-Five electoral votes from Florida that became issued to George Bush, Jr. I think the electoral process is a way to eliminate voter fraud and return power and authenticity to the states. I think the voter recount in Florida did not undermine the polling process but was only used to demonstrate accuracy. I think the basic argument with voters is that the popular vote does not always win the presidential election. Voters feel that their opinions are lumped together with misrepresentation in the presidential election, especially with winner-take-all policy. I think that citizens need voter security when addressing political issues. I believe voters felt uneasy when Bush won, especially after Gore won the popular vote. I do not see why the 2000 election was scrutinized, but I can say I think it was due to legal action taken by the candidates to determine the authenticity of American voters. I think it is rare to see a political race become decided on electoral votes and not on popular votes. However, I do think the Electoral College system presents possible laws. As our population increases, the number of electors per state rarely reflect the population changes. I also believe that the presidential election should have more weight on the popular vote. The popular vote reflects more toward American thinking. Our nation is built upon popular vote, and popular vote covers participating voters that should be relied upon in-dividual opinion. We as citizens have a right to be heard. More people will be pleased with coverage based upon the popular opinion.

As citizens', popular votes occur in each part of our lives, as chil-dren we vote for student government at school, mock presidential elec-tions at school, and even as we go into college/adulthood, where the same type of system is used. It is hard to discern the way we elect presi-dents. While I understand we use the Electoral College, reform needs to happen to accommodate the citizens' choice for president.

I think that the Electoral College needs reform. Many states have population changes that have not increased or decreased the Electoral College voters. According to U.S. Government Info, there are many states where both electoral votes have either increased or decreased based on population changes; however, in my mind there is no sig-nificant way to discern how the change effects polling. One way the

Electoral College could benefit from reform would be to allow the system to reflect population changes.

When learning about reform of the Electoral College, there is a wonderful nonprofit organization whose mission is to help have every vote count. Fairvote.org supports three main points to voting, which include, "Fair access to participation: We support universal voter registration, a constitutionally protected right to vote and education preparing youth for their role in our democracy. Fair elections: We support a national popular vote for president, instant runoff voting for single-winner and more transparent and accountable election administration. Fair representation: We support choice voting and other methods of proportional voting for local, state and national elections" ("Fair Vote"). The mission uses the word *transparent*. Transparency is a word that is much underused in today's society. If we were to reform the Electoral College, we would be displaying a sense of transparency within our community. This openness would, in turn, be a valuable lesson for the younger population to embrace and learn.

Since I have just entered my early thirties, there has been a cause for extensive research on this topic since I was almost too young to remember the various details of the election of 2000. A *Time* article printed back in 2000 gives some great background that this was not the only election where electoral votes were not always looked upon as great for our society. Schlesinger states, "The abolition of state-by-state, winner-take-all electoral votes would speed the disintegration of the already weakened two-party system. It would encourage single-issue ideologues and eccentric millionaires to jump into presidential contests." We need to go back to square one and just let the popular vote win. This contest would ensure that the presidential candidate that receives the most votes would prevail and lead our country.

I believe when citizens' ideas and opinions lack representation due to changes based upon population size, US presidents lose political meaning and duty for US citizens. I think that was a problem with the 2000 election. The 2000 presidential election went against popular opinion. I do not think the presidential election was damaged, but I do think the citizens should examine the process in which we do elect our presidents. Elective examination means taking a closer proactive look to understand the election process. There are many reform organizations with information on many websites that can assist one in gaining meaningful knowledge about the process.

In conclusion, the presidential election is the most important position to run for in the US. The entire world looks on to our country when we have the election for president every four years. We have due diligence to enter into elections with proper intentions clear purposes for citizens and the ability to show every vote counts. We as citizens have a duty as vital members of this country. When we vote, we are showing that we care and pick a side where we believe that an individual candidate for president is aligning with our beliefs. I leave you with this quote I came across from Cynthia McKinney: "In November 2000, the Republicans stole from America our most precious right of all: the right to free and fair elections…Now President Bush occupies the White House, but with requalified legitimacy".

The President & The Power

In today's modern institutional era, I believe the president has less power than in the past. Several "monumental" events occurred, which I believe has shaped the power of the presidency today. It is evident that the country has changed over the course of time, and in time the power of the presidency has shifted. If we as a society do not embrace the changes that have occurred, the power of the presidency will continue to diminish.

The underlying job of the president is "to be the leader of our country, to represent the peoples' opinion, protect our country, advice committees/leaders, appoint leaders, sign or veto bills, and make agreements with others." In a special done on PBS, it was said, "From 1789 to 1828, the United States government and its presidents functioned, for the most part, the way the Founders intended. A change began with the election of Andrew Jackson in 1828. He was the first president to think of himself as the head of democracy and claimed that he was the one to best represent the will of the people since-after all-only he had been elected by all of the people."

Throughout many years, there have been substantial changes in the dynamics of the country. These changes are critical times in our development as a country. To comprehend and analyze them, we must look at several events of changes throughout the past to best summarize the diminishing power of the presidency.

From Watergate of 1972 to the Clinton scandal of 1998, there has been a shift of power because of the choices presidents in the past have made. After the Clinton scandal, presidents are demanded by the citizens to be more accountable and transparent. The actions of the president must be justified to the citizen to portray a popular position in office. In the textbook *Understanding the Presidency*, it states that there are three types of accountability the president must be able to demonstrate. The three categories are "ultimate, periodic, and daily accountability." If we hold presidents accountable, it will cohesively strengthen the powers of separation.

The powers of the modern president go beyond the perception of the framers. Franklin D. Roosevelt implemented the contemporary presidency. Authors Pfeiffer and Davidson describe the contemporary presidency best as: "Institutionalized by his successors, presidents acquired any tool

to work around their constitutionally mandated weakness. They used their formal powers strategically and proactively; they built an executive branch in their image, with extensive presidential staff to oversee and control it; and they continually and creatively interpreted constitution vagueness in their favor to reshape the policy landscape, relying on a direct connection with the public to legitimize their action." Modern presidency encompasses mostly various duties as described below. It takes not only an incredible person with superb discipline and diligence but also some who envision what the country should look like and how it should work.

The 1970 resurgence regime has eroded, and presidential power has expanded to fill the void. All modern presidents highlighted the idea of "inheriting" presidential power. The broad sweep of the constitutional rights of the office. "The modern president has potent tools and a global reach unforeseen by the architects of the constitution." A globalized, polarized world seems to call out for endowing leadership sufficient to match its powers to the tasks at hand.

There are many constraints that I see within the presidency. It is important to realize that times have changed, and with the changing times come new restrictions. In my opinion, the president faces challenges and limitations. Some examples include the fiscal budget, political party differences, and job description developed by the founders of the constitution. In general, presidents may process and create procedures established for the office that does not allow the president to act "out of the box."

The separation of powers is a constraint of the executive because the Supreme Court is the only set of people allowed to interpret the constitution. The system of check and balances established by the framers of the constitution acts as a constraint on the executive office primarily affecting the president.

It is apparent in my opinion that the office of the presidency has been increasingly less powerful throughout the course of time. With our country growing and expanding as rapidly as it is, an article I found best represents my perspective of how the presidency is less powerful in today's era. On a website entitled "American History: from Revolution to Reconstruction and beyond, the compilations of information break down the history of the presidency. The website states.

"The president finds that the machinery of government operates pretty much independently of regulatory interventions, has done so through earlier administrations, and will continue to do so in the future. New presidents get immediately confronted with a backlog of decisions from the outgoing administration on issues that are often complex and unfamiliar. They inherit a budget formulated and enacted into law long before they came to office, as well as major spending programs (such as veterans' benefits, Social Security payments and Medicare for the elderly), which are mandated by law and not subject to influence. In foreign affairs, presidents must conform to treaties, and informal agreements negotiated by their predecessors."

The First "100 Days" in Office

F ranklin D. Roosevelt's First Hundred Days was the most effective and influential presidential policy the US had ever seen. The Hundred Days of 1933, borrowed from French history, became the most prosperous time spent with Congress on legislation. The US was suffering from financial disaster and growing national depression. FDR took office on March 4, 1933, with the promise of a strong presidency. FDR's One Hundred Days is an important example of policy leadership because it mended the relationship between central government and the United States citizens. Banks were failing during this period. People were losing their life savings. Businesses became short of cash. FDR reacted with a sense of urgency. Within three months of a special session held in Congress, he bargained through sixteen significant bills. These sixteen bills became known as the New Deal. The significance of the Hundred Days is important because he created sixteen bills in the first one hundred days in office. No other president before his time has surmounted a growing public fear with a plausible feat in the The United States.

In the book *Understanding the Presidency*, the authors state, "In the three months after Roosevelt inauguration, Congress and the country were subjected to a presidential barrage of ideas and programs, unlike anything I knew about American history." The Hundred Days is an important example because FDR led and enacted fifteen significant laws, delivered ten speeches, held press conferences and cabinet meetings twice a week, conducted talks with foreign heads of state, sponsored an international conference, and made all domestic and foreign policy decisions. FDR was also a charismatic leader. FDR was able to connect with many almost instantaneously. FDR brought new energy to people who had lost faith in the central government, and the central governments abilities to solve problems while in crisis. FDR was a legislative success.

The Hundred Days differs from other presidential experiences because of conditions produced by the Twentieth Amendment, the character and timing of congressional "honeymoons" with newly elected presidents and ignorance about the ways and means of some institutions.

The Twentieth Amendment was designed to end the four months of lame duck status to meet in regular session on January 3 of the year after November's election. The new timing was disadvantageous for new presidents. During FDR's era, presidents had four months before the inauguration to choose their cabinets. Instead, the new Congress is in session three weeks before the commencement awaiting the new president's initiatives.

In contemporary time, the congressional reflection of a public "honeymoon" has not lasted for more than six months. The "honeymoon" period is a time of new initiative for the president when he selects his cabinet and his advisors. The novelty of office is still nostalgic for newly elected presidents. Typically, this differs from FDR's Hundred Days honeymoons. At best honeymoons decide a president's success with legislation. Since the time of FDR, there has not been a more successful president for legislative success within a honeymoon period.

The Hundred Days differs from other presidents' experiences because of contemporary ignorance. If the newly elected president has not held executive office, he will be ignorant of many things he needs to know and can learn only by experience through the hundred days. This is a part of the presidency that has changed since FDR's Hundred Days. FDR's Hundred Days was an appropriate use of presidential leadership. Harold Ickes wrote "It's a new world. People feel free again. They can breathe naturally. It's like quitting a morgue for the open woods." Winston Churchill wrote, "Roosevelt is an explorer who has embarked on a voyage as uncertain as that of Columbus and upon a quest which might conceivably be as important as the discovery of the New World." Roosevelt was a leader. His Hundred Day legislation made him a stand up the president. Once in office, FDR immediately took charge of the administrative office. FDR maintained a level of accountability and responsiveness to leadership. "FDR invented the modern presidency during the depression and WWII." The push for an honest and hard-working president is a model of the modern president. FDR's Hundred Days is an example of hard and focused work. The US citizens sought after an accountable president during the depression and the world war.

In my mind, FDR was able to bounce back from adversity. In several articles I read, he was a person who kept trying to find the correct solutions. I think we all can agree the office of the president is stressful and many times unproductive because of all the cynical politics that are involved with both parties. FDR showed the citizens of the US that with charisma and persistence, things could be accomplished.

Elite Selection

The framers of the constitution created an effective office when they developed the executive branch and the office of the president.

Ten out of forty-four presidents have contributed to the greatest successes of the US federal government. The framers of the constitution set aside laws for the executive branch to function in a central government. The constitutional role of the executive branch has been itemized into executive powers that serve as guidelines for administrative operations. Many have been elected, but only a quarter represent an effective executive office that the framers of the constitution intended to serve. The development and elected powers of the president have made few presidents successful. The president is described as "both the head of state and head of government of the United States of America." They are also named the commander-in-chief of the armed forces. The president gets appointed by the citizens of the US and is "responsible for the execution and the enforcement of the laws created by Congress." In the US, there are fifteen executive departments. These departments are led by an appointed member of the presidential cabinet to coordinate various aspects of the president's mission. The president also appoints the heads of more than fifty independent federal commissions. The direct executive office of the president consists of the immediate staff of the president.

The president encompasses the ability to either sign legislation or to veto bills proposed by Congress. "The executive branch conducts diplomacy with other nations, and the President has the power to negotiate and to sign treaties that must be ratified by two-thirds of the Senate. The President has unlimited power to extend pardons for federal crimes. In my opinion, the president is charged by citizens to uphold a moral and ethically sound job. Not only is the president given complete control of the US, but they also must work with other nations to ensure the safety of the country.

The presidential candidate must meet specific eligibility requirements to run for office. The requirements are stated in the constitution. The three requirements are: "the president must be 35 years old, be a natural born citizen, and have lived in the United States for at least fourteen years." To become the president of the United States, the candidate must be nominated to run for office by the Electoral College. The Electoral College consists of 538 electors who nominate a presidential candidate. The presidential office is limited to two four-year terms.

In my opinion, many fantastic, influential, and diverse men have occupied the office of the president. The men who have held the presidency have overcome many obstacles and have immensely developed our country into a real cohesive nation. I have narrowed down a list of the top presidents who have displayed the "job description" created by the framers of the constitution.

1. Richard M. Nixon—"was successful at ending the war in Vietnam. He also contributed to the improvement and restored the relationships with U.S.S.R and China. President Nixon had some major accomplishments during his Presidency, which included revenue sharing, the end of the United States military draft, new anticrime laws, and the establishment of a broad environmental program. While under his presidency the United States space program was able to make its first landing on the moon." President Nixon acted as a very diligent ambassador for the United States.

2. Woodrow Wilson—"created three significant pieces of legislation; the Underwood act, child labor laws, and the Versailles Treaty. The Underwood Act lowered tariffs and produced a progressive federal income tax bill. Child labor limited working hours to be eight hours a day. The Versailles treaty comprised of fourteen points aimed to establish a general association of nations affording mutual guarantees of political independence and territorial integrity to great and small states alike." I think that Woodrow Wilson's presidency

established the current worldview for Americans. The Versailles Treaty established an independent nation free and clear from internal and external forces.

3. Ronald Reagan—"created a program called Reagan Revolution that aimed to invigorate the American people and reduce their reliance upon the government. Reagan created legislation to stimulate economic growth, curb inflation, increase employment and strengthen national defense. Reagan produced legislation that created many deductions and exempted millions of people with low incomes. The Nation enjoyed its longest record of peacetime prosperity with recession or depression." Reagan's foreign policy achieved "peace through strength." The government increased its defense budget by 35 percent in addition to resolving issues between US and Soviet relations. Reagan negotiated a treaty with Soviet leader Gorbachev that would eliminate intermediate-range nuclear missile attacks. He also declared war against international terrorism by sending bombers against Libya. Reagan naval escorts protected the free flow of oil during the Iran-Iraq war. Reagan is an excellent choice for the top ten because he established national as well as international policy. Reagan embodies a capitalist ideology.

4. Lyndon B. Johnson—"In his first years in office, he passed one of the most extensive legislative in American history. He led in the struggle to eradicate Communist encroachment in Viet Nam. He served as a Navy Lieutenant commander during WWII. During Johnson presidency, Johnson employed 'The Great Society Program' a National program to clean up the United States. Johnson had a clear vision to develop his agenda. Congress rapidly enacted Johnson's recommendations. Johnson provided aid to education, attack on disease, Medicare, urban renewal, beautification, conservation development of depressed regions, fight against poverty, control and prevention of crime and delinquency, and the right to vote."

5. Winner-by-popular-vote, Andrew Jackson—" Andrew Jackson was a steward of the US constitution. As President, he sought to act as a direct representative of the common man. Jackson was the first

man elected from Tennessee to the house of reps. Before his in- auguration, Jackson was also a major general in the war of 1812. Jackson was named old Hickory. Jackson is important because the two parties' system grew from Jackson having office. The two party systems emerged from Jackson in office. The United States two- party systems; consists of democrats and republicans."

6. George Washington—"took oath as the first President of United States. Washington mastered military arts and western expansion. 1754 he was commissioned a lieutenant colonel. He fought dur- ing the French and Indian war. In 1775 Washington was elected Commander and Chief of the Continental Army. Washington be- came more important leading up to the Constitutional convention. The Electoral College elected Washington as President. Washington was very influential his presidency was effective at leading the colo- nists to freedom from Britain."

7. Franklin D. Roosevelt—"Helped the American people keep faith during the great depression. He stated, 'The only thing to fear is fear itself' to improve national morale. When Roosevelt was elected, 13 million people were unemployed. In his first 100 days, Roosevelt enacted recovery for business, agriculture, and relief for the un- employed who became endangered of losing farms, homes, and reform. As part of the national change, Roosevelt created social security, more massive taxes for the wealthy, new controls for banks and public utilities, and work relief for the unemployed. During his second election, he was able to sanction regulation for the economy. Roosevelt led during the attack on Pearl Harbor by organizing re- sources for global war. President of Presidents developed national and international diplomacy that everyone accepted as President. He led during a difficult time. American morale was at a low and Roosevelt was an ability to rally with an American interest at favor."

8. Abraham Lincoln—"as President built the Republican party into a strong national organization. In 1863, he issued the Emancipation Proclamation that declared to set slaves free within the Confederacy. Lincoln states during a cemetery dedication in Gettysburg, "that we

were here highly resolve that these dead shall not have died in vain, that this nation, under God, shall have a new birth of freedom, and that government of the people, by the people, for the people, shall not perish from the earth." Lincoln had a strong public opinion that despite southern opposition, he envisioned a stronger confederation. Lincoln is one of the influential Presidents because he is responsible for winning the American Revolution and emancipating the slavery."

The framers of the constitution created an active office when they developed the executive branch and the office of the president. Eight of forty-four presidents have contributed to the success of the US federal government. The framers of the constitution set aside laws for the executive branch to function in a central government. The constitutional role of the executive branch has been legislated into executive powers that serve as guidelines for presidential operations. The top eight most influential presidents according to me have significance, but only a quarter represent an effective executive office that the framers of the constitution intended to uphold constitutional supremacy.

Diversity and Inclusion

I can honestly say that I have learned a tremendous amount of information in the category of "diversity and inclusion." I thought that with my background of having a son with autism and working in special education I already had a vast knowledge of the course. I realized quickly that I had a surface knowledge of what "diversity and inclusion" actually meant within the context of special education. The new knowledge has impacted my life, and I can attest to the information I have gained.

I can define diversity as a heterogeneous mix in society working for a common goal. Diversity includes relationships with all races, nationalities, ethnicities, economic, social, disabled, and religious affiliate things mixed for the common good. A diverse mixture of students provides ideas, insight, and problem-solving. Diversity can be found in the classroom, workplace, religious institutions, and in the real world. I think the more diverse a society becomes, the more likely it is that society finds connections between others not of the same background. I can define inclusion as a good faith action to accept persons for their differences and work together for all goals for qualifying persons even with inequity. Special needs kids are a contemporary example not only for inclusion but also exclusion. They can participate with a mainstream integration by learning and achieving in a less restrictive environment. People feel included when they belong to a group of their particular interest. Students feel included when they can ask questions about life and do not get rejected but encouraged to think and to respond.

The BLAST (Bible Learning Adventures & Story Time) is a children's church where they learn about Jesus and Christian morals the church presents to each child. The church demographics are of white upper-class suburban college-educated citizens. The students act more inclusive than exclusive. My concern with BLAST is that the small number of children who attend the program is substantially lower than I had anticipated. A small number of church families who have children are just not bringing themselves to church. My Church has a small congregation, and I think that a decrease in church membership now and in the future will put my Church to a disadvantage based upon the regional church-going population.

I found a comparison between Philadelphia public schools versus suburban schools in disparity. Suburban schools are more affluent than the city kids. The only problem is that church membership is at a low. Many families that attend my Church are upper-class home-owning citizens. The church is located along the mainline stretching from Coatesville to Philadelphia. Crime is very low in this suburban region. Property taxes are very high. Suburban school districts have access to the best technology, business districts, real estate, and resources that encourage inclusion. The majority of the suburban population is of Caucasian descent. My Church is a local example of affluence (Bush).

At the beginning of the class, the children were allowed to run around for the first fifteen minutes. Many of the kids get restless, so free play is encouraged. The age range is between three and twelve years old. My job was to observe the lesson activities prepared by the BLAST teacher. The children learned about the golden rule written in Luke 6:31. This verse was introduced to provide moral support of the golden rule. The children reacted with obedience. The BLAST teacher also taught to love your enemy. During this lesson, the children gave more attention. The children learned to do good to their enemies. Christians must have faith to operate with morals within norms and values. The children learned to love and express gratitude. They demonstrated good listening skills throughout the lessons.

Overall, the children seemed to interact as though they are mainstreamed in education. The children acted as if they accepted each other. The children were very inclusive. The children did not participate in much exhibition or competition. The children seemed to get along, especially with my son Cayden who is black and white or biracial. I first thought the kids would group up, especially with the oldest male child acting unruly. All children demonstrated good listening skills and participated in group activities. I believe the children are too young to stereotype each other. Overall, I learned kids could be as dedicated to church as their parents.

I think the children at my Church practice concerted cultivation; a tool to get a competitive advantage in the world. The kids participate and play along with each other but do not practice free play in the neighborhood. The church has a budget to accommodate and facilitate each child to participate in the BLAST program. Each BLAST season requires two hundred dollars per month to run the program. I think the church members provide these contributions to keep kids off the streets, free play and provide support to families in the community. Each lesson is prepared and organized by the BLAST teacher. Formal instruction takes place during the BLAST hour. BLAST requires student attendance logs to officiate the program.

The students help one another. For example, the oldest female student poured the water for her fellow BLAST students. I think most of the students participate in after-school activities like sports and music. Students in BLAST make lifelong friends and are encouraged to be a part of the youth group. Students who attend church are more likely to be studious and focused on secondary education and also extending into undergraduate programs. Free play is not encouraged, but structured learning is the key to success.

Students learned to pray together and to love one another. In the world of secularism, people contacts are hard to make and manage due to a lack of common belief, shared experiences, and social inequity. Free play seems to be an example of secularism. Neighborhood rules for free play get created by children based on brawn and power versus education and a sense of community.

Learning about the second class, I want to focus on the second classroom about the BLAST program. The BLAST program is an example of an excellent second classroom. The BLAST children all share a universal religion that is not learned in the nearby and local public schools. They are encouraged to share, practice, and believe in the Church doctrine. Even throughout the common American nationality.

Each child has a different point of view concerning American education. Outward faith in religion is discouraged in nearly every public school, but expressing an opinion in faith-based second classrooms encourages a child to have a unique social identity. Kids can rely on faith and share stories about their own experiences. BLAST allows students to fellowship, build, and instill faith-based leadership models.

BLAST girls started to help cut out materials for the lesson. The church is a second classroom where a mixture of grade, sex, ethnicity, economic status, and skill levels teach students to communicate with each other within their societal identity. Through GOD, one can do everything. The students can release, fellowship, or worship with students who might not go to the same school or are in the same grade level. BLAST creates a sense of excitement. The students must respect and praise with stories, music, activities, and games that instill religious ideology. There is a relationship between adult spiritual worship and offspring worship. Both are children of God and are expressed from the sanctuary to the academic and to the secular world.

We started BLAST, and as usual, the students practiced esteem-building practices. Everyone acknowledges each other and learn to get along. I want to focus on my son, Cayden Price because he is the mixed student to BLAST. Without knowing him personally, one would not know that he has autism. I have observed Cayden about the reading on special education. I am learning about laws that govern special needs children. I have firsthand experience with Cayden and autism, of course, as well as a special need child I once taught.

My son is a student who has a disability. He is diagnosed with Autistic Spectrum Disorder. I learned about "eight bits of intelligence" that empower students not only support our children in the community but also teach parents to approach the eight bits of intelligence with confidence and with direction toward autism. If Cayden could set goals based upon the "eight bits of intelligence," he will improve his frame of reference and his understanding of the world. Teachers also need to emphasize the importance of teaching the eight bits of intelligence so that students have a better chance of survival and human flourishing.

Cayden is good with logical mathematic intelligence. He works well with numbers. He can solve problems logically and scientifically. Cayden has an appropriate level of verbal communications skills for his age. Cayden does not express himself well enough to be understood about spatiality, but he can build train track design with "outside the box" thinking. Cayden develops moderately toward a strong visual intelligence. Cayden is very sensitive to nature. He liked to play in the dirt. He loves making muddy waters for his Thomas the tank engine trains. I also think Cayden has strong intrapersonal skills. He carries a sense of pride in himself. He does not let others influence him and he understands right from wrong, and he carries himself this way. Doctors say that Cayden will have a tough time to connect socially due to his autism, but so far so good. Cayden has been able to learn in a community that provides support toward his education as well as his social well-being.

Regardless of race, ethnicity, nationality, gender, and cultural differences, students can apply the four types of knowledge to build a diplomatic approach to public education and inclusion. I think the start of multicultural education should begin with a second classroom environment. Each student should share with classmate's cultural background that defines a social identity and develop each student's world perspective. I think the second classroom should be the first objective to introduce students to a multicultural environment of inclusion. If teachers and students follow Banks' rule in a multicultural setting, the public education system for multicultural environments develops a competency and ethic to encompass multicultural learning inside and outside the classroom. Banks best talks about the connection of personal knowledge, popular knowledge, mainstream, academic knowledge, and transformative knowledge that teachers must involve to function not only in a multicultural classroom but also in global perspectives.

I believe group work and collaborative learning support academic learning as a means to develop strong academic skills inside and outside the classroom. Students who engage in open-ended questions are encouraged to solve problems in a 3D world through collective collaboration and inclusive approaches toward the problem. The benefits of a collaborative approach for students welcome multi-talents and intelligence as a new set of eyes for a solution. Multi-dimensional approaches allow students to learn and achieve not only by one-dimensional thinking but also by spherical or global expressions to develop results and answers inclusively in a real-world application. Students can make significant contributions outside of the one-dimensional world into a round approach to group assignments. Student accountability in a group establishes faith and trust for every group member's actions.

It is imperative that we as a society embrace and convey the importance of diversity and inclusion. Many times when items are not "talked" about or relayed as an essential lesson for our children, we also stop supporting what we believe. This class has increased my awareness and knowledge of being an integral part of implementing diversity and inclusion in my family/work life. It is evident that we do this for the betterment of society and our children. We need to be mindful that our children are the future.

Works Referenced

Bush, Tehron J., *Class Reaction Journals*. 2013.

Zehr, Howard. *Changing Lenses: A New Focus for Crime and Justice*. 3rd ed. Scottdale: Herald Press, 2005.

Bibles, Zondervan. Pew Bible-KJV-Large Print. Zondervan, 2010. Print.

Cavanagh, Michael E. *Before The Wedding, Look Before You Leap*. Westminster John Knox Press, 1994.

Peck, M. S. *The Road Less Traveled: A New Psychology of Love, Traditional Values, and Spiritual Growth*. 25th Anniversary ed. New York: Touchstone, 2003.

Scott, Kieran, and Michael Warren. *Perspectives on Marriage, A Reader*. New York: Oxford University Press, USA, 2007.

Supplementary Notes-Kosnik's Human Sexuality.

Gau, James V. *Successful Marriage*. Pastoral Psychology 60.5 (2011): 651–58.

Winter, D.D., Leighton, D.C. (2001). Structural Violence. In D.J.Christie, R.V.

Wagner, & D.D. Winter (Eds.). *Peace, Conlict, and Violence: Peace Psychology in the 21st Century*. New York: Prentice-Hall.

Jaffee, Martin. *Torah. Encyclopedia of Religion*.

Conaty, Bill, and Ram Charan. *The Talent Masters: Why Smart Leaders Put People before Numbers*. New York: Crown Business, 2010.

Kidder, R. M. How Good People Make Tough Choices (pp. 30–176). New York: William Morrow & Company, Inc., 1995.

Kouzes, J. M., & Posner, B. Z. *Credibility* (pp. 1–118). San Francisco, CA: Jossey-Bass, 1991.

Kidder, R. M. *Overview: The Ethics of Right versus Right. In How Good People Make*

Tough Choices Resolving Dilemmas of Ethical Living (p. 24). New York, New York: William Morrow and Company, Inc., 1995.

Kidder, R. M. *Right Versus Right: The Nature of Dilemma Paradigms. In How Good*

People Make Tough Choices Resolving Dilemmas of Ethical Living (p. 113). New York, New York: William Morrow and Company, Inc., 1995.

Hook, Steven. *US Foreign Policy. Presidential Power.* Sage Publications, 2010.

Piffner, J. & Davidson, R. *Understanding the Presidency.* New York: Pearson, 2009.

Works Cited

El Fadi, Fathi M. "Sudan and Darfur: The problem is political." People's Weekly World Newspaper, June-July 8, 2006. http://www.pww.org/article/articleview/9287/1/325/ (accessed September 17, 2009).

"Divorce." Wikipedia. Wikimedia Foundation, 15 Dec. 2012. Web. 16 Dec. 2012.

"National Islamic Front." Wikipedia. http://en.wikipedia.org/wiki/National_Islamic_Front (accessed October 8, 2009).

New World Encyclopedia. S.v. "Sudanese civil war." http://www.newworldencyclopedia.org/entry/Sudanese_civil_war (accessed October 8, 2009).

Sudan. "The Reasons of the Conlict in Sudan." Panorama. http://www.tigweb.org/express/panorama/article.html?ContentID =4270 (accessed September 14, 2009).

"Sudan: History, Geography, Government, and Culture." Infoplease. http://www.inforplease.com/ipa/A0107996.html (accessed October 12, 2009).

"Sudan People's Liberation Army/Movement." Wikipedia. http://en.wikipedia.og/wiki/Sudan_People's_Liberation_Army/Movement (accessed October 8, 2009).

Beschloss, M., & Sidney, H. (2009). The presidents of the United States of America. Retrieved from www.whitehouse.gov (All Presidential Biographies are from Whitehouse.gov) 5/6/2013

Walsh, K. (2009, February 12). The first 100 days: Franklin Roosevelt. US News. Retrieved from http://www.usnews.com/news/history/

articles/2009/02/12 the-first-100-days-Franklin-Roosevelt-pioneered-the-100-day-concept

Byker, C. (Producer). (n.d.). Andrew Jackson: Good, evil & the presidency. [Web Page]. Retrieved from http://www.pbs.org/kcet/andrewjackson/features/power_presidency.html Web. 12 Nov 2012. <http://college.cqpress.com/sites/hook/Home/chapter4.asp&xgt;

How powerful is the American president?. (2008, November 10). The Week with First Post. Retrieved from http://www.theweek.co.uk/25253/how-powerful-American-president

Welling, G. (1994, November). Constraints on presidential power. Retrieved from http://www.let.rug.nl/usa/outlines/governmeant-1991/the-executive-branch-powers-of-the-presidency/constraints-on-presidential-power.php

"Electoral Votes by State in 2012." About.com US Government Info. N.p., n.d. Web. 03 Oct. 2012. <http://usgovinfo.about.com/od/thepoliticalsystem/a/2012-Electoral-Votes-By-State.htm>.

Fairvote. (n.d.). Retrieved from www.fairvote.org

Schlesinger Jr., A. (2000, November 20). Electoral College debate: Election 2000. Time, \ Retrieved from http://www.time.com/time/printout/0,8816,998527,00.html http://ind.galegroup.com.ps2.villanova.edu/gvrl/infomark.do? &content Set=EBKS&type=retrieve&tabID=T001&prodId=GVRL&docId=CX3424503139&source=gale&userGroupName=vill_main&version=1.0. (accessed October 25, 2009).

Jewishfaq.org. "Torah." Judaism 101: Torah. http://www.jewfaq.org/Torah.htm (accessed October 25, 2009).

"The Torah." The Torah-History & Facts. http://bethhamashiach.com/what_is_Torah.htm (accessed October 25, 2009).

"Befogged Vision: International Environment Governance a Decade After Rio." LexisNexis Academic. http://www.lexisnexis.com.ps2.villanova.edu (accessed December 8, 2009). "Biotechnology Is Ineffective and Potentially Disastrous." Gale Cengage Learning.

http://ind.galegroup.com.ps2.villanova.edu (accessed December 8, 2009).

"The United Nations at a Glance." United Nations. http://www.un.org/en/about/index.shtml (accessed December 8, 2009).

At a glance. (n.d.). Unicef-Ghana. Retrieved September 11, 2010, from http://www.unicef.org/infobycountry/ghana_statistics.HTML?q=printme

At a glance. (n.d.). Unicef-United States [Statistics]. Retrieved September 11, 2010, from http://www.unicef.org/infobycountry/usa_statistics.html

A repository of all districts in the Republic of Ghana. (n.d.). Ghana Districts. Retrieved September 11, 2010, from http://www.ghanadistricts.com/home/?_=60&sa=5446

"United Nations Conference on Population and Development." Gale Cengage Learning. http://ind.galegroup.com.ps2.villanova.edu (accessed December 8, 2009).

"United Nations Conference on Women." Gale Cengage Learning. http://ind.galegroup.com.ps2.villanova.edu (accessed December 8, 2009).

"United Nations Convention on Conventional Weapons." Gale Cengage Learning. http://ind.galegroup.com.ps2.villanova.edu (accessed December 8, 2009).

"United Nations Convention on Terrorism." Gale Cengage Learning. http://ind.galegroup.com.ps2.villanova.edu (accessed December 8, 2009).

"The United Nations Must Reform Its Management Practices." Gale Cengage Learning. http://ind.galegroup.com.ps2.villanova.edu (accessed December 8, 2009).

"U.S. Actions in the War on Terror Have Damaged the United Nations Peacekeeping Power." Gale Cengage Learning. http://ind.galegroup.com.ps2.villanova.edu (accessed December 8, 2009).

"Responsible Parenthood." Natural Family Planning Program, n.d. Web. 16 Dec. 2012. <http://www.usccb.org/issues-and-action/ marriage-and-family/natural-family-planning/catholic-teaching/ upload/Responsible-Parenthood.pdf.

www.ingramcontent.com/pod-product-compliance
Lightning Source LLC
Chambersburg PA
CBHW051538120626
46551CB00013B/1271